THOMAS WOLFE

Modern Literature Monographs

THOMAS WOLFE

Fritz Heinrich Ryssel

TRANSLATED BY HELEN SEBBA

Frederick Ungar Publishing Co.
New York

Translated from the original German and published by arrangement with Colloquium Verlag, Berlin

Contents

Chronology

1900: 3 October: Thomas Wolfe is born in Asheville, N. C.

1904: Mrs. Wolfe moves temporarily to St. Louis for the World Fair, taking her children with her.

1912–15: Tom attends the private school run by J. M. and Margaret Roberts. Tom has a paper route.

1916–20: Attends University of North Carolina at Chapel Hill. Becomes a member of F. H. Koch's Carolina Playmakers.

1918: During summer vacation works as time checker at Langley Field and on the docks at Newport News, Virginia. Tom's brother Ben dies.

1920–24: Attends Harvard. Participates in George Pierce Baker's Workshop 47.

1922: Receives M.A. degree. Wolfe's father dies.

1923: *Welcome to Our City* is unsuccessfully produced at Harvard.

1924–30: Works intermittently as assistant instructor in English at Washington Square College of New York University. Travels and works in Europe. First trip is in the fall of 1924. Rewrites *Mannerhouse* in Paris.

1925:   Meets Aline Bernstein on return voyage.

1926:   Travels in England with Aline Bernstein.
          July: Begins his first novel, *Look Homeward, Angel*.

1927:   Asheville real-estate boom collapses.

1928:   Is involved in a fight at the Munich Oktoberfest.

1929:   Meets Maxwell Perkins. *Look Homeward, Angel* is published.

1930:   Receives Guggenheim fellowship. Spends several months in Europe.

1931:   Relationship with Aline Bernstein is finally ended.

1932:   *A Portrait of Bascom Hawke*, a short novel, is published.

1931–34: Devotes himself to writing in Brooklyn.

1933:   December: Perkins encourages Wolfe to finish the manuscript of *Of Time and the River*.

1935:   Second novel, *Of Time and the River,* is published. *From Death to Morning* is published.

1936:   Attends Olympic Games in Berlin on his last trip to Europe. Is troubled by friction with Perkins and Scribner's. *The Story of a Novel* appears.

1937:   Close to nervous collapse, Wolfe visits New Orleans. Meets William B. Wisdom, who buys his papers and manuscripts after his death. Signs contract with Harper's, which gives him a ten-thousand-dollar advance on his next book, sight unseen.

1938:   February: Wins lawsuit against dishonest agent. Perkins testifies for him. Leaves manuscript with Edward C. Aswell for first reading.
          May: Makes speech on "Writing and Living" at Purdue University.

May–June: Takes strenuous rail and automobile trip through the west.

4 July: Travels by boat from Seattle to Vancouver. Becomes ill.

11 July: Pneumonia is diagnosed. X-rays at Seattle hospital disclose lung lesion.

12 August: Is taken by train to Baltimore.

12 September: Brain operation discloses miliary tuberculosis.

15 September: Wolfe dies without having recovered consciousness.

1939:   *The Web and the Rock* is published.

1940:   *You Can't Go Home Again* is published.

1941:   *The Hills Beyond,* a collection of short pieces and a fragment of a novel, is published.

In Retrospect

Something indefinable surrounds Thomas Wolfe's personality and the tremendous oeuvre he produced with such furious haste in little more than ten years, like a man with a vital message which he must deliver before nightfall. "If I had but a hundred years there might be some realization of my dream," he wrote to his mother. "I will not hesitate to say what I think of those people who shout 'Progress, Progress, Progress.' . . . In the name of God, let us learn to be men, not monkies."[1]

This sort of language and attitude is apt to inspire confidence in those who seek new directions and reject outworn conventions and principles. Wolfe's determination to live up to his word earns him the trust of every new generation, beat, angry, or whatever. His work represents more than literature. It is a program, something to hold on to in time of trouble and despair. His wounds authenticate him.

Thomas Wolfe was a wanderer and a genius, who drove himself until he collapsed. He took life in giant strides. "And dark time is feeding like a vulture on our entrails, and we know that we are lost, and cannot stir

. . . and there are ships there! there are ships! . . . and
Christ! we are all dying in the darkness!"[2] He dedi-
cated his whole life to communicating his vision of "the
great dream of time." He brought a whole continent to
life. This was his object wherever he found himself: in
his native North Carolina, in New York City, on his
many visits to Europe, on journeys across his own and
foreign lands. Constantly he was pursuing and pursued,
driven by the need to allay his homesickness, to find the
rescuing, liberating word, to find a meaning in so much
meaninglessness. Hence the fervent plea which runs
through his work like a refrain: "Look homeward,
angel."

Home, the haven, tranquility, the magic door, the
father—these are the landmarks on the psychological
chart of the early and the late Wolfe. Where did he find
support and gain admittance? Where is home? Which
road leads to the goal, back into childhood, the past,
and time remembered? "You can't go home again."
Wolfe's titles are ciphers symbolizing his own development and experience, cover names for victories and de-
feats sustained in endless struggles. His journey began
with accusations, indictment and revolt. It ended in
renunciation of the desire to know everything, in loneliness, yet also in hope. Having gained experience and
insight in a bitter struggle with his own self, Thomas
Wolfe abandoned his pursuit of his early vision: "to be
famous and to be loved."

No neat formulation of his personality or writing
really works. More to the point is Schopenhauer's remark that genius cuts across the regular path of the

planets like a comet, following a completely eccentric course of its own. One side of Wolfe loved life and dreaded "silence" and "darkness"; the other spoke of the hour when we shall be allowed to enter into the heart of love. He worked with the energy of a great dynamo, driving himself as though he were inexhaustible, and he died at thirty-eight. He wanted to take in the whole world, and yet, as the dying man in "Dark in the Forest, Strange as Time," one of Wolfe's short stories, whispers, "Vun field, vun hill, vun riffer, . . . zat iss enough!"[3]

When Scribner's reader, the poet John Hall Wheelock, asked him what the title of this short story— "Dark in the Forest, Strange as Time"—meant, Wolfe could not explain it. Image and sound carry the meaning. He saw man's wretchedness as well as his mysterious greatness—"the beast with the swine-face and the quenchless thirst, the never-ending hunger" as well as "the strange and powerful music of the soul."[4] He annoyed uncompromising "patriots" by pointing out America's weaknesses, its hustling and money-grubbing, yet he dreamed of the golden future. His merciless criticism ended on the note of "the promise of America." He sought God and eternity but never called them by name.

A man prepared to "slay hunger and beat death" could not falter when it came to resisting the pressure of convention. There was a human price to pay, and Wolfe paid it. Literary critics and journalists said he had no sense of structure, could not plan a book and keep it within bounds. After his death in 1938 they

came to understand that, as he once said himself, everything he wrote was part of one single book—of what he
called "the book." Looking back, his friend and editor,
Max Perkins, was able to distinguish the architectural
concept behind the great oeuvre. There were no plans
—only the sureness of Wolfe's conception. One won-
ders whether some day the published works may not be
rearranged, the tremendous parts reassembled in a new
order, the individual books integrated into "the book."

"But it would be hard to get Tom right," Max
Perkins said to Elizabeth Nowell, Wolfe's friend and
literary agent, when they were discussing a possible
biography of Wolfe, even before his death. His prophetic words still hold good. Wolfe himself wrote to his
mother in 1924: "I don't think I have ever quite understood myself, and I have never found anyone who understood. That's why I'm lonely."[5] As time passed, he
acquired a better understanding of himself and the
world, but there were still plenty of contradictions. A
sense of humor did not preclude self-pity or self-re-
proach. He would fight with his publishers over one
half of one percent if he thought they were cheating
him, yet he despised haggling and stinginess because
"of all the forms of human ugliness, money-ugliness is
the most hateful and most damnable, and when it gets
into families, there is hell to pay."[6] He extolled the
magic of the big city, yet later described the cold heart-
lessness of "the rock."

After a visit to Asheville, his home town, in 1937,
he realized that he could never go home again. As a
young man he dreamed of success and fame; later he

saw that there could be "no rest," and relinquished the happiness he had yearned for. He never allowed himself a pause to sit back and enjoy what he had accomplished. As he well knew, the interval between books is one of the worst things in a writer's life. "It is really hell, or worse than hell, because writing itself is hell, and this period of waiting is limbo."[7]

He did not understand himself, but he acquired some self-knowledge. "What I am trying to tell you, what I am forced to say because it is the truth, is that I am a righteous man, and few people know it because there are few righteous people in the world."[8] He was a deeply religious man, who made no secret of his doubt. His sense of self decreased as his sense of life grew. As he discovered the world, he turned to the humiliated and the reviled. Like his fellow American William Faulkner, he believed in the future. A few months before his death he wrote to his sister Mabel: "To be afraid is also defeat."[9]

1

Plays—
And an Epic
Touch

Thomas Wolfe's letters, edited by his literary agent Elizabeth Nowell and published in 1956, present a complete scenario of his life, with all the suffering, the pride, and the greatness of this puzzling man. Letters to his family, friends and fellow students, to Margaret Roberts, a former teacher who meant a great deal to him, to Maxwell E. Perkins, his friend and editor at Scribner's, and to Edward C. Aswell, his last editor at Harper's and his literary executor, provide a detailed record of his thoughts and inmost feelings. John S. Terry, Wolfe's friend from their college days in North Carolina, edited his letters to his mother—a rich source of information about his life and the mother-son relationship.

Terry, who saw a lot of Wolfe during his New York years, was commissioned to write a biography, but when he died in 1953 he had not gone beyond the preliminaries. Elizabeth Nowell, who had edited the letters with skill and tireless attention to detail, was able to expand his notes into a reliable, carefully researched biography that constitutes a sound basis for the study of Wolfe's life and work. Written after the death of most of the key figures, it presented many new details and relationships.

"Each of us is all the sums he has not counted: subtract us into nakedness and night again, and you shall see begin in Crete four thousand years ago the love that ended yesterday in Texas. . . . Each moment is the fruit of forty thousand years. The minute-winning days, like flies, buzz home to death, and every moment is a window on all time."[1]

Thomas Wolfe was born on 3 October 1900, to William Oliver Wolfe, a stonecutter, and his wife Julia E. Westall, a well-known and respected real-estate broker and proprietor of the Asheville boarding house known as the Old Kentucky Home. His first novel, *Look Homeward, Angel*, gave his parents a permanent place in American literature under the names of Oliver and Eliza Gant. Recent research has shown that his forebears were of Pennsylvania Dutch, English, and Scotch-Irish origin. Julia Wolfe was over forty when Tom, the youngest of her eight children, was born. From her he inherited his incomparable memory, his delight in storytelling, and his tenacity in pursuing a goal; from his father his sense of artistry and "the heart of a wanderer."

His mother was a self-assertive woman whose feet were firmly planted on the ground and an infallible judge of character. "I believe I could have been a writer myself," she said to Terry, "if I'd had a little more training. Tom thinks he knows a lot about people's characters. Humph! He's as easy to fool as anybody else! But they can't fool me."[2] Wolfe once told her that one half of him was great fields and mighty barns and the other half the great hills of North Carolina. His father, born in 1850, was originally from Pennsylvania and had moved south, then up to the mountains, during his years as an apprentice and journeyman. "There has never been anybody like Papa," Wolfe wrote after his death.

It was Wolfe's mother, not his father, who agreed to send him to Harvard for a year. When he visited his parents in Baltimore where his father was in a hospital, they promised him a second year, and after his father's death in 1922 (the unforgettable scene is recorded in *Of Time and the River*) his mother sent him back for a third one. A successful play would have made things much easier, promising a certain degree of independence (Tom's years at Harvard had used up his share of his father's legacy) and a decision about his immediate future.

As a student (from 1916 to 1920 at the University of North Carolina, Chapel Hill, and from 1920 to 1924 at Harvard) Wolfe's mind was set on dramatic laurels. At Chapel Hill he was a member of Frederick H. Koch's Carolina Playmakers, and at Harvard he participated in George P. Baker's famous Workshop 47, which was a rich source of new talent for the American theater. Full of both hope and despair, earning applause as well as unfavorable criticism, Wolfe devoted himself whole-heartedly to playwriting, until he finally realized that this was not the medium best suited to his talents. Koch gave his enthusiastic student a recommendation, and Baker, the great authority, thought highly of him. How was he to know that Wolfe had not yet found his true vocation? And yet he must have suspected it, because in 1923 he commented that the first act of one of Wolfe's plays had "an epic touch."

On 15 May 1923, Baker's Workshop performed *Niggertown* or, as it was later entitled, *Welcome to Our City*. It was the most ambitious production the Workshop had ever attempted, with ten scenes, a cast of more than thirty, and seven different sets. The play deals with the attempts of a group of real-estate brokers, acting in collusion with the town authorities, to buy up advantageously located property in the black section of a town. In letters to his mother written at this time Wolfe disparaged and ridiculed these arrogant men and their money talk, who could become extremely unpleasant when their own or other people's money was at stake. Although these newly rich are always talking about their principles—"the principle of law and order"—right means no more to them than an empty word. Their speculative plans for new subdivisions arouse the resistance of the black community, led by the impressive figure of Johnson. There is a riot, and the National Guard ruthlessly restores order—or what the authorities call order.

The story would have made a good play in the hands of the right dramatist. Wolfe, however, wanted to present a complete cross-section of the life of the town, and as a result many characters and much of the dialogue are irrelevant to the action. A stage director's function is to cut, not to blunt dramatic effects. Professor Baker recognized his student's gifts—his marked sense of detail and his talent for developing subsidiary characters—but he pointed out to him that the novel would provide more scope for what he wanted to do. A penciled note in the margin of Wolfe's one-act play *The Mountains* suggests that he is using a novelist's technique. The extensive stage directions and character descriptions that precede the first act of *Welcome to Our City* validate this criticism. A girl from Asheville anticipated the reaction of many critics and fellow citizens

when she remarked with dismay after the first performance that she recognized every character in the play.

Wolfe's weakness—attempting too much and trying to say everything there was to be said—was already
causing him trouble as a dramatist, although in his
youthful exuberance he still thought the energy he
brought to his work would overcome all difficulties.
"Some day I'm going to write a play with fifty, eighty, a
hundred people—a whole town, a whole race, a whole
epoch—for my soul's ease and comfort," he wrote to
Professor Baker.[3] *Welcome to Our City* was only his
"second fusillade" in a lifelong battle against the hollow pyramid of a hypocritical social order.

For Wolfe as a writer *Welcome to Our City*
marked a step forward on the still uncertain road. It
was like the tuning of an instrument. Social criticism
and satire were recurring features of his fiction. The
rejection of shallow notions of progress was to be
among his permanent themes. The disturbingly evil figure of Governor Preston Carr was intended to expose
the true nature of a hypocritically blustering personality. Wolfe's surely poised pen made telling sketches of
the career-minded professor, the stupid delegate of the
woman's club, the smooth preacher who walks out of
the crucial meeting called by the callous businessmen,
who are now determined to resort to force, muttering
meaningless phrases such as "Faith, faith, my brothers.
... Yes, and tact."

But one of that band of wanderers who invoke the
angel and seek the door walks quietly past the loud-
mouthed bosses, listening for "lost music under sea."

This is the consumptive poet Jordan, a relative of Gant. Others in the band are Gant himself, Ben, and Eugene. Jordan's friendly relations with the lawyer symbolize a spiritual kinship.

As an individual, old Rutledge serves as a dramatic foil to Johnson, but psychologically and spiritually he does not act as a counterforce. Where dramatic construction requires that there be an antagonist to Johnson there is just another man: the conflict-torn Rutledge. He even gives up his plan to buy back his parents' house when he realizes that this would mean making common cause with the brutal bosses of the power structure, the false prophets of progress, and the churchgoing conformists.

Wolfe too knew what it meant to be conflict-torn. It took time for him, born a Southerner and forced into prejudice by background and custom, to overcome it entirely. He never intended the play as a contribution to the black question. As he explained to his cousin Elaine Westall Gould, all he was trying to do was to "give a picture about a certain section of life, a certain civilization, a certain society."[4] That was all.

With the perceptivity he occasionally displayed, Wolfe took a look at his situation and recognized its limitations. Friction with Professor Baker may also have had something to do with it. In 1922 he was ready to withdraw from Harvard, but decided to complete the year and take his master's degree. The appointment office had found him a position as instructor in English at Northwestern University. "The conviction has grown on me that I shall never express myself dramatically. I am therefore ending the agony by the shortest way; I would not be a foolish drifter promising myself big things," he wrote to Professor Baker.[5]

Such were his thoughts in March 1922. Nevertheless, he stayed on. Professor Baker encouraged him, and he wrote an expanded version of *The Mountains.* Instead of tightening up this one-act play—for it was already obvious that cutting was not his line—he turned it into a three-act play. He also had some hope that a successful Workshop production of *Welcome to Our City* would give him a start on Broadway. This had happened to other members of the class. But the success he hoped for never materialized although *Welcome to Our City* is his best play. What are the reasons for its failure? Probably its length, its failure to concentrate on a single theme, and technical defects in the performance itself, which dragged on until midnight.

Wolfe lacked the true playwright's dramatic instinct. In the lecture delivered at Purdue University a few months before he died, he offered the following descriptive yet accurate analysis:

Something in me, very strong and powerful, was groping toward a more full, expansive, and abundant expression of the great theater of life than the stage itself could physically compass: it was something that had to come out sooner or later, as a pent flood bursts above a dam—and in 1926 I found it—and another cycle had been passed, another period of development begun.[6]

Writing to Professor Koch to tell him that he did not wish his early play *The Return of Buck Gavin* (published in *Carolina Folk Plays*) to be republished, Wolfe took a historical view of his early Playmakers period: "I was a boy of eighteen years when I wrote those plays, and I wrote each of them in a few hours because I did not then understand what heart-breaking and agonizing work writing is . . . and I think those plays show this."[7]

Wolfe himself considered *Mannerhouse* his best play. The manuscript had an eventful history but was eventually published in 1948.

Leaving Harvard and Professor Baker, Wolfe went to New York. Although he was not yet aware of it, he was on his way, though he still thought of himself as a dramatist. The parting was painful. He did not get a Workshop prize for *Welcome to Our City*. In December 1924 the New York Theater Guild turned the play down and advised him, as everyone in the Workshop had done, to shorten and tighten it. He did not do so. Instead, he applied for a position in the English department of the Washington Square College of New York University.

This was the beginning of a new phase in his relationship to his mother, his family, and the South in general: a move toward independence in daily life and toward inner freedom. A projected play about his family remained a one-scene fragment. In 1924 he was still waiting for the creative impulse, the flood that would overflow banks and barriers.

He wrote a frank assessment of his personality and qualifications to Homer A. Watt, chairman of the English department at New York University. An unfinished article by Professor Watt shows that his honesty had its effect. Wolfe instinctively trusted other people;

his later reserve and mistrust were the outgrowth of insinuations, slander, and lawsuits. He tended to underestimate rather than overestimate himself:

I am twenty-three years old and a native of Asheville, North Carolina. I do not know what impression of my maturity my appearance may convey but it is hardly in excess of my age. In addition, my height is four or five inches over six feet, producing an effect on a stranger that is sometimes startling. I think you should know so much in advance, as the consideration may justly enter into any estimate of my qualifications.[8]

He assured Professor Watt that he would give the most faithful and efficient service he was capable of. Between 1924 and 1930 he taught at New York University intermittently. At those times he devoted himself unstintingly to his teaching and to the correction of "damned freshman themes" and stacks of blue books. In October 1924 he made his first trip to Europe, leaving behind drudgery, disappointments in the theater, and long nights of writing, to follow the wake of ancient cultures and draw closer to the novel.

He left Harvard without saying goodbye to Professor Baker. At sea he wrote him a letter, which the friend to whom he entrusted it never delivered—a conciliatory, fair, and appreciative letter. Anger and exasperation over future plans and the uncertainty of existence had vanished. This ability to see the past in proportion enabled Wolfe to portray both friends and enemies not as distorted caricatures but in dense, lifelike character sketches as inventive as Balzac's.

One result of this trip was a new version of *Mannerhouse*. This came about because the concierge of a small hotel in Paris lost a suitcase containing some shabby clothing and the only existing manuscript of *Mannerhouse*. This play was based on a story Wolfe's father used to tell about the South at the time of the Civil War and reconstruction. The owner of the house, a typical Southern aristocrat, is living in a changed world, unaware of time, unaware that a new order has replaced the old one. According to the story, he passively sells his vast estate for a pittance to an up-and-coming lumber dealer. In one of the aristocrat's two sons, Eugene, "a mighty epic struggle" between tradition and insight is being fought out. Here we have Wolfe's great theme of the tireless struggle to find the right road. Returning home after an absence of many years, Eugene tears down a column of the house and is killed in the wreckage.

The conflict-full play, which is often emotional, and sometimes didactic, sparkles with Wolfean poetry and rhetoric. Which side is Wolfe on? Does he speak for the good old days or for the new South? For neither. The old generation and the old South are played out. This is "the pitiful story of the decay and disintegration of a family"—and of a social order grown sterile. The new masters are not masters in any real sense; the land is "given over to thieves, carpet-baggers, Negroes." In 1920 or 1921 Wolfe was considering a different, more optimistic ending. As "glorious forerunners of the new South" Eugene and Christine would settle down on a little plot of ground. "We are not living in the Memory of past greatness, but Now and Here."[9]

Mannerhouse is a cryptic, indecisive play, includ-

ing both criticism and confession, dealing with thoughts
and themes that would recur later in Wolfe's work: the
rebel, the South, the life of a house and a family. Its
melodic language sets a tone which, skillfully cultivated
by Wolfe, grows stronger and more distinct with the
years.

EUGENE (*from the darkness*): No, General. Not more light—
more warmth! Men do not die of darkness, but of cold.

GENERAL: I have believed for all my days in what could not
be seen—in smoke, in some perhaps; in hidden faith, and secret
honor, in all the beauty and the mystery in the hearts of men.

EUGENE: Some day. Who knows? The roads lead back if we go
far enough.[10]

We do not know why Wolfe did not proceed with
the hopeful ending. Perhaps his distaste for the new
type of businessmen and money-grubbers was so strong
that he inwardly took the side of the noble dreamer
estranged from life. This play, he wrote to Alice Lewisohn, director of the Neighborhood Playhouse in New
York City, "contains the first complete expression of
that thing that has fascinated and terrified me since I
was a child. Are we alive or dead? Who shall tell us?
Which of the people in this play are ghosts, and which
are living?"[11]

As for literary influences, we may turn to the passage in *Of Time and the River* in which Eugene Gant
makes his hesitant comments on his play before reading
it to his friends at their house on the Hudson River:

From this description, it will be seen how the young man's play
was made up both of good and bad, how strongly it was marked

by the varied influence of his reading and idolatry—by Shakespeare, Chekhov, Shaw, Rostand, the Bible—and how he had also already begun to use some of the materials of his own life and feeling and experience, how even in this groping and uncertain play, some of the real grandeur, beauty, terror, and unuttered loveliness of America, was apparent.[12]

Much in *Mannerhouse* marks the transition to Wolfe's later work: references to contemporary events, satirical passages, the indictment of hypocrisy and dishonest business practices and of callous, grasping middle-class materialism. Wolfe had already begun to use the "great, inimitable stuff of life" in a particular form. "The speech of Porter was the plain, rich, pungent, earthy, strongly colored speech of his mother, of his uncle William Pentland, and of the Pentland tribe."[13]

A deep-lying current of religiosity pervades the entire work of Wolfe, this stranger, this wanderer who heard a voice and heeded it.

In the letter to Alice Lewisohn already referred to, Wolfe wrote:

I am a young man who read the Greeks at 15, and who read Kant and Hegel at 17, and who, like every other fool, thought himself wise when he saw God as a sea, himself as a drop of water on the way; but who knows now, at 25, that he had merely substituted an ugly superstition for a beautiful one.[14]

In France in 1924 Wolfe was overcome by homesickness. The America from which he had fled was irresistibly calling him back. On foreign shores he discovered to what country and under what sky he really belonged. He enjoyed traveling, looking at cities, women, rivers, streets. He had gone to Paris to work in the belief that an artist might find a happier life there than in America. In *The Story of a Novel* (1936) Wolfe was to describe his stay in Paris and his discovery that most young Americans were trying to escape not the philistinism and ugliness of American life but "the necessity of finding in ourselves, somehow, the stuff to live by."[15]

Wolfe now began briefly to erupt, producing his first prose works: memoirs and impressions. Homesickness precipitated "a stream of blazing pageantry across my mind, with the million forms and substances of the life that I had left, which was my own, America."[16]

He was also acquiring first-hand knowledge of the world and felt himself becoming more mature—despite a confused, mercurial love affair, which brought him both pain and ecstasy, with a Boston girl he had met through his friend Kenneth Raisbeck (Professor Baker's assistant, who would later figure in his work as Starwick).

The discovery, in Europe, of "his" America showed Wolfe a goal toward which he was to strive as though pursued by furies. "I saw that I must find for myself the tongue to utter what I knew but could not say . . . and my life would ache with the whole memory of it; the desire to see it again, somehow to find a word for it."[17] On his journey home he wrote to his mother from London: "I know that I have something to say now; it twists at my brain and heart for expression. If God would only give me a hundred hands to write it down."[18] In England he was ill for three weeks

—"more dead than alive." (At college he had already suffered alarming episodes of blood-spitting.)

On the return trip from Europe in 1925, the twenty-five-year-old Wolfe met Aline Bernstein—the Esther Jack of the novels—on whom his whole life was to center for the next five or six years, in spite of jealousy, rage, quarrels. Nineteen years older than Tom, Aline Bernstein was the wife of a New York businessman and the mother of two grown daughters. Through her work as a stage designer she knew all the celebrities of the theatrical, literary, and publishing worlds. This woman became Wolfe's muse, standing by him through depressions, nervous collapses, and crises of self-doubt. She even took the affairs of his daily life into her competent, skillful hands. His mother in Asheville, hitherto the ruling sovereign, felt that her youngest child was at the threshold of becoming irrevocably independent of her. As Elizabeth Nowell said, her economic and psychological hold over him was broken; their relationship, though it survived, was never the same again. "Mrs. Wolfe's baby was getting away from her."

Wolfe later wrote of Aline Bernstein: "Esther was fair; she was fair; she had dove's eyes."[19] He said that after getting to know her he began to feel compassion for all the poor blind creatures that inhabit the earth— something that had never occurred to him when he was twenty "because young people are thoughtless and cruel."

The year 1926 was a turning point. True, the Neighborhood Playhouse did not accept *Mannerhouse*, the play Wolfe had rewritten in Paris; his mother lost money on a real-estate deal in Florida; and the great depression, still unrecognized by most people, was already in the offing. Wolfe went home for a visit, although, as he said, the invitations had been neither cordial nor frequent.

On 23 July 1926 he embarked on the *Berengaria* for his second voyage to Europe, and in July wrote to Margaret Roberts that he had begun a book, a novel, which he was thinking of calling "The Building of a Wall." (He stated—perhaps intentionally—in *The Story of a Novel* that he started this project in the fall.) In London he joined Aline Bernstein, who had brought James Joyce the royalties from the production of his play, *Exiles*. In a dark hallway Wolfe caught his first glimpse of Joyce, whose work had inspired his own new start.

Aline provided Wolfe with big ledgers to write in, and on a green hillside, in the warm sunshine of a July afternoon, he began *Look Homeward, Angel*. "It was a moment of intense and solemn inspiration for him, and he told her that he would be a great writer and that long after she was dead people would know about her because she would be 'entombed in his work.'"[20] The woman who had become his friend, mother, adviser, and mediator with the world generously undertook to finance his stay in England while he was working on his novel. When she returned home, he wrote on alone.

Time and again he thought his novel near completion, but he did not reach the end until March 1928— in a tiny apartment Aline had found for him in New York. He would work from midnight until the early hours of the morning, then sleep for a while before setting to work again. Twelve to eighteen cups of coffee a day helped to keep him going. Aline Bernstein cooked for him; sometimes they went out for a meal together. He still had neither agent nor publisher, until Aline took matters in hand. Then he began to receive rejection slips; he was advised to make cuts. Embarrassed and extremely depressed, he returned to Europe—without his friend.

With characteristic acumen and tenacity Aline Bernstein sent a carbon of the manuscript to the critic Ernest Boyd. He passed the voluminous work along to his French wife, Madeleine, who was just getting started as a literary agent. She liked it and sent it to Maxwell E. Perkins, senior editor of Charles Scribner's Sons, and editor of Fitzgerald, Hemingway, and, in his later years, James Jones. In the fall of 1928 Perkins wrote a friendly letter to Wolfe, who was still in Europe, asking him to come and see him. On 1 January 1929, Wolfe, who had been hospitalized in Munich after getting into a fight at the Oktoberfest, presented himself at Scribner's and came away with a signed contract and a check for five hundred dollars.

2

Behind the Wall: Look Homeward, Angel

Perkins was prepared for Wolfe's visit. The manuscript of *Look Homeward, Angel,* the characterization of Eugene, and the reports that had reached him of the fight at the Munich Oktoberfest had told him what to expect. At first sight Wolfe reminded him of the young genius Shelley. Wolfe for his part found Perkins "not at all 'Perkinsy'—name sounds Midwestern, . . . but very elegant and gentle in dress and manner."[1] Nine years later, after quarrels, a change of publishers, and a reconciliation, he wrote his last letter to this intimate friend and father figure—a very moving letter tinged with a premonition of death.

Perkins stood by him in trouble and despair, giving unstintingly of his time and help. From 1926 to 1937 Tom respected and trusted him in the most crucial matters. Driven by his compulsion to write, Wolfe could not achieve the reliable overall view of his work that Perkins gained from the position of "a skilled observer at a battle." We have no reason to doubt Wolfe's self-critical ability, but the fact remains that during those years he did his best work when he sat down with Perkins and sorted out his material, systematically cutting and reorganizing it.

It took months of work to turn the shapeless manuscript into a publishable book. In his application for a Guggenheim fellowship Wolfe wrote that they had cut more than a hundred thousand words, reducing the twelve-hundred-page manuscript to a more suitable length. Perkins sensed that this unusual, vital book had some sort of inner unity, though not in the orthodox sense of having a formal structure that complied with the conventional rules. The unity he saw "came from the strange wild people—the family—it wrote about, as seen through the eyes of a strange wild boy."[2]

Look Homeward, Angel, published in 1929, is pervaded by Wolfe's longing to be delivered from suffering and restlessness. It is a book about the home-sickness of the stranger, in the Platonic sense. Old Gant, a stonecutter, dissolute, hard-drinking, full of pathetic complaints, has never learned to carve a smile on the face of a stone angel. All his bluster and fuss cannot hide his need to express something obscure and inexpressible. Sensitive Ben detects in his younger brother Eugene dreams and yearnings that are all too familiar to him. "He bore encysted in him the evidence of their tragic fault: he walked alone in the darkness, death and the dark angels hovered, and no one saw him."[3]

The working titles Wolfe chose reflect personal and literary influences and summarize the growth of his mind and spirit—chapter headings, as it were, in a psychological biography. "The Building of a Wall"—the original working title for *Look Homeward, Angel*—suggests that the boy and the young man, seeking protection from the hostile world around him, would like to withdraw behind a wall. The title symbolizes the hero's struggle toward "an essential isolation; a creative solitude; a secret life." Eugene Gant is fiercely intent upon walling off his inmost feelings, his vulnerable self, against the world, "first against the public and savage glare of an unbalanced, nervous brawling family group; later against school, society, all the barbarous invasions of the world."[4]

In September 1927 Wolfe wrote the line "O lost,

and by the wind grieved, ghost, come back again"—a line that might almost be called the leitmotif of *Look Homeward, Angel*. At this time he was thinking of calling this book "O Lost." The title under which the manuscript was published—*Look Homeward, Angel*—was taken from Milton's "Lycidas," a pastoral monody written at the death of a friend.

"Young Poseidon," "Poseidon's Harbor," and "Theseus" are allegorical titles that show the influence of James Joyce. "The Hills Beyond Pentland" commemorates a view of the North Carolina mountains and Wolfe's relationship to his mother's relatives, to whom he gave the fictional name of Pentland. This was the working title of his last, unfinished book about his mother's family. "Alone, Alone" is a reference to "The Rime of the Ancient Mariner" by his favorite poet, Samuel Taylor Coleridge, and to the world of English romanticism. "We are all strangers upon this earth we walk on. . . . naked and alone do we come into life, and alone, a stranger, each to each, we live upon it," he wrote to Margaret Roberts.[5]

Such was the genesis of this "story of the buried life," the epic of the Gant family, a tremendous portrait of American life and of one particular landscape. Hermann Hesse called it the most powerful contemporary American writing he knew, and Wolfe himself said that the most exact thing in it was the fantasy—the picture of a child's soul.

In this first novel of Wolfe's saga, this story of a struggle between man and wife has the inexorability and greatness of true tragedy. The subject matter of a small-town novel has been wrought into a new structure. The man and the woman collide like natural forces, "the one with an inbred, and also an instinctive, terror and hatred of property; the other with a growing mounting lust for ownership that finally is tinged with mania—a struggle that ends in decay, death, desolation."[6] The detailed description of twenty years in the life of a forceful family has been worked up into a relentlessly harsh, honest book, full of unspoken understanding and lyrical protest. Even in what he called "this wilderness of ugliness and provincialism" Wolfe could see "beauty and spirit which will make us men."[7]

Wolfe defended and explained his aims in a "Note for the Publisher's Reader," which he intended to send out with the manuscript that was to become *Look Homeward, Angel.* The book, he said, has in it sin and terror and darkness, "ugly dry lusts, cruelty, a strong sexual hunger of a child." And yet Wolfe wrote it "with strong joy, without counting the costs, for I was sure at the time that the whole of my intention—which was to come simply and unsparingly to naked life, and to tell all of my story without affection or lewdness—would be apparent."[8]

In Wolfe's psychological makeup, a strong personal motive for the writing of this book can be detected. The son of a family was rebelling, taking stock, setting himself free. Subject and palette had long been ready, as Tom's letters to his mother show, especially a letter fragment of May 1923 in which he wrote about consciousness and memory and said, "And I intend to

wreak out my soul on paper and express it all." Then in
1925 Aline Bernstein entered his life, with her understanding of the slights and sorrows of childhood and
youth, and encouraged him to realize his plan. We
begin to understand what Wolfe meant when he said
that the book "represents an enormous excavation in
my spirit."[9]

Remembering how the hurts of childhood rankle,
we should not be surprised that his wounds were slow
to heal. He told Margaret Roberts that life at home—
"that hell of chaos, greed, and cheap ugliness"—had
become practically impossible for him after his brother
Ben died. "I was without a home—a vagabond since I
was seven—with two roofs and no home."[10] Then,
during his adolescence, came a long period of depen-
dency. While he knew that his mother had always had
her children's welfare at heart, he also knew that she
was sometimes slow to recognize necessity—"sometimes too late—sometimes to the tune of clods of
frozen earth upon a wooden board—the last venture in
real estate . . . any of us will ever make."[11] Making no
attempt to embellish "the simple brutal truth," he reminded his sister that "I got away because I had to get
away, there was no place for me at home."[12]

Which of us has known his brother? Which of us has looked
into his father's heart? Which of us has not remained forever
prison-pent? Which of us is not forever a stranger and alone?
. . . Remembering speechlessly we seek the great forgotten language, the lost lane-end into heaven, a stone, a leaf, an unfound
door. Where? When?

O lost, and by the wind grieved, ghost, come back again.[13]

When Ben died, Eugene was left all alone—Eugene whose true nature was now completely enshrined in the very center of his imagination. And Ben? "Like Apollo, who did his penance to the high god in the sad house of King Admetus, he came, a god with broken feet, into the gray hovel of this world."[14] The soul has intimations of its origins in another realm. In "Ode on Intimations of Immortality," Wordsworth expressed Plato's ideas of its preexistence. Wolfe, an admirer of Coleridge and Wordsworth, began the epigraph of *Look Homeward, Angel* with the refrain "a stone, a leaf, an unfound door" without explaining it. By means of this he evoked recollections of the immanent within the visible. Angelic language and angelic music. In his vision Eugene slowly mounted the long wooden steps. As he reached the top, he saw that the man was Ben.

The reception of *Look Homeward, Angel* in Asheville, and the South in general, was a source of anger and distress to Wolfe for many years, causing him a long exile. He set great store by the opinion of his friends and fellow Southerners. Unfortunately they took *Look Homeward, Angel* for the documentary story of a town and threatened to lynch him. School friends and acquaintances charged him with "spitting in the face of the South." His "damned book" read so authentically that one family claimed to have recognized the stone angel (nonexistent in Asheville) on a grave. Margaret Roberts, his revered teacher and mother figure, resented her appearance as a caricature and stopped writing to him from 1930 to 1936. Tom's mother, however, was proud of her youngest son and of his first novel.

The critics' charge that Wolfe was incapable of writing anything but autobiography (or what they saw as autobiography) disturbed him for years and influenced him too.

Writing is more than just getting material down on paper. When Wolfe acquired patience, he tried to clear up the misunderstandings. To his uncle Henry A. Westall, and to the rest of the family, Wolfe explained the artist's functions in simple terms: "I know that you will understand this: an artist does not work in order either to praise, wound, insult, or glorify particular people—he works in order to create some kind of living truth which will be true for all men everywhere."[15] He justifiably maintained that he created living characters of his own—"a whole universe of my own creation. And any character that I create is so unmistakably my own that anyone familiar with my work would know instantly that it was my own, even if it had no title and no name."[16] Later, in a more relaxed and humorous mood, Wolfe could dismiss his critics' rankling charges by saying that while there was no harm in describing a horse thief, it wasn't necessary to give his address and telephone number.

Sinclair Lewis (who received the Nobel Prize in 1930) openly praised the young writer's work, saying that Wolfe dealt with the whole of life and that if he kept up the standard he had set he might well become America's greatest writer.

Before Wolfe even began to write about looking for a father, he had found one. The father of his writing and his revolt was James Joyce. Joyce's example loosened Wolfe's tongue. His self-confidence impressed this young man, who was fighting his own shyness and awkwardness. Melville's dictum—woe to him who tries to save himself at the expense of the truth—linked Joyce and the early Wolfe. The indebtedness Wolfe failed to express when he happened to meet Joyce at the battlefield of Waterloo and in Frankfurt in 1928 he acknowledged later in *The Story of a Novel.* Speaking of writers he admired who might have influenced him, he singled out only one: James Joyce. "Like Mr. Joyce I wrote about things that I had known, the immediate life and experience that had been familiar to me in my childhood."[17]

Dublin and Asheville—both beloved, never to be lost, yet out of reach. Specialists in Joyce, Wolfe, and contemporary literature in general have convincingly documented Joyce's influence on Wolfe (if, indeed, any documentation was needed), pointing out borrowings, imitations, echoes of themes and motifs, similar methods of describing a stroll through a town or of handling a stream of consciousness, lists, tricks of word order, the structure of interior monologue, a way of speaking with the dead. These are all offshoots of Joyce's *Ulysses,* outgrowths of *Portrait of the Artist as a Young Man.*

Certainly "The Web of Earth" in *From Death to Morning,* a story that Perkins admired for its flawless self-contained unity, could never have been written without Mollie Bloom's monologue, which comes at the end of *Ulysses.* Yet its rhythms and subject matter are Wolfe's own. There is no mistaking his mother's tone of voice, the thoughts and attitudes of the mountain folk,

Asheville local history, memories of the Gants and the
Pentlands. Perkins considered "The Web of Earth" a
great work.

"In the Park," another story in *From Death to
Morning*, recalls turn-of-the-century New York, when
Esther's father, an actor and artist, was still living.
Here Wolfe tried to find through Aline Bernstein's ex-
perience a key to bygone days, the door, meaningful
existence itself.

Wolfe drew away from Joyce, wanting to write his
own "Ulysses," but he did not forget "to pay the tribute to
a man of genius that is due to him."[18] The search for a
father points back to Joyce, although we should not
forget that as a young man Wolfe had already dealt
with the father-son theme in *Mannerhouse*.

As time went by, Wolfe was to draw away from
his first novel. Older and more mature, though by no
means more conservative, he no longer felt at home in
the role of youthful hero, full of romantic pathos, protest, and indignation. He was to look back with a critical eye. The self-judgment he arrived at in *You Can't
Go Home Again*, though not to be taken literally, is
certainly no pose. By that time he had reached the
point of overestimating Joyce's influence, to the extent
that he saw himself as dependent on Joyce. Perkins
overlooked this relationship and called him a great
writer.

Before leaving to live in Europe on a Guggenheim
fellowship in May 1930, Wolfe made a will. He was not
yet thirty, but, as he fatalistically said, one never
knows. His possessions—little enough "except books

and manuscripts and some royalties waiting at Scribner's"—were to be divided equally between his mother
and his "dear friend, Aline Bernstein." (A later will left
everything to his mother and made Max Perkins his
executor.) In fact Wolfe parted from Aline Bernstein
when he went to Europe to live this time. On his return
she took an overdose of drugs and was ill for a long
time. A reconciliation was followed by a final break.
Aline once made a suicide attempt in the editorial
offices at Scribner's. On 1 April 1931, Wolfe wrote to
his mother that he had been considerably worried over
a friend who had been in the hospital, apparently with
some sort of collapse. In June, soon after his mother
had visited him in New York, he told her that he was
"at peace with everyone, as well as free and heart-
whole," although in the next sentence he mentioned a
certain intelligent young woman. At about the same
time he was speaking retrospectively of his love for
Aline, who, he said, was old enough to be his mother.
That summer he wrote to a girl about the passion that
had obsessed him for years. By then he was hard at
work in Brooklyn.

Aline Bernstein came to terms with Wolfe in short
stories of her own. Wolfe resented her portrayal of him
as a dreamer. Having once threatened to sue his publishers for infringement of privacy, she now, as a woman
scorned, did just what she had threatened to prevent
Wolfe and his publishers from doing. Yet during
Wolfe's final illness she talked to him on the telephone.
She could not understand the change in the dying man's
voice and thought he had been drinking. After his death

she wrote proud letters of reminiscence to Wolfe's biographer, Elizabeth Nowell.

Why did the relationship end? Elizabeth Nowell too stresses the age discrepancy. There were conflicts, and perhaps ideological and political differences. And finally love was its own enemy: "the terrible invasions of love which rob men of their unshared secrecy, their deep-walled loneliness, the soaring music of their isolation."[19]

When Wolfe realized to what extent love could exclude everything else, absorbing all his thoughts and energies, he told himself that he was paying too high a price, "and he began to fret and chafe against the shackles that his heart had forged." That is how he saw it in *Of Time and the River*. The separation may also have been due to other unacknowledged factors—and to his own idiosyncrasies. As a young man he tried to find in his friends the poise and self-confidence that he himself lacked, yet at the same time he was constantly scrutinizing them for their weaknesses. A preconceived idea of what a person should be like kept him aloof from the people around him. When crises occurred between him and his friends, he would indulge his tendency to analyze everything over and over again, until he wore people out. He once drove Perkins to exclaim: "If you have to leave, go ahead and *leave*, but for Heaven's sake, don't talk about it any more!"[20]

When he returned from Europe in 1931, Wolfe buried himself in the "vast sprawl" of Brooklyn. Even if this meant breathing "the seventy-nine stinks of Brooklyn," he no longer had to breathe "the unutterably fouler stink of *la vie littéraire,* as practiced in this noble city." Feeling that he could no longer work in the glare of publicity, he was safeguarding his privacy. In Brooklyn he was "free, finished, deserted, left gloriously alone by the last son of a bitch of an autograph collector and gossip writer." He had found out "what a piece of stinking fish the literary racket is."[21] A table and paper to write on were all he wanted. What went on around him did not bother him. He lived in his work, mulling it over until he penetrated to the core of it. Furnishings, pictures, curtains, rugs did not matter to him; he never even noticed them.

John S. Terry, Wolfe's college friend, has described Wolfe's Brooklyn apartment. In the bedroom were a cot, a battered old bureau, and a straight chair. The cot looked uncomfortable, but it was long enough to accommodate Wolfe's six feet six. Books and papers were scattered all over the place. The telephone was on the mantelpiece, along with piles of old letters. The most important object in the room was an old packing case standing on the bare floor. This "dry goods box" was a Wolfean legend.

It held large bundles of pencilled and typed manuscripts, ledgers, and other accretions of the years of Tom's writing. No one except Tom ever touched this material. It sounds unbelievable, but he could reach his hands down into this great mass and after a while, in an uncanny way, find the desired bundle.[22]

Wolfe treasured and carefully preserved drafts and sections of books—themselves often as long as an average book. He would transpose, revise, rewrite—or simply let them lie there in the famous box, rejecting anything that did not meet his standards.

From Brooklyn Wolfe wrote to Sinclair Lewis that he was working away, but "whether I am as good as the material is another thing."[23] Contrary to all expectation, this unbroken spell of work lasted almost five years—five years of anguish and despair. His next book, *Of Time and the River*, appeared in 1935.

3

Of Time
and the
River

Wolfe's second book—and his fears that his candle might have burned out—caused him plenty of trouble. He knew that he had the material for a hundred books, and the superabundance often made him feel uncertain and pressured. He had no firm plan, and in any case planning was not temperamentally natural to him. In a letter to the Guggenheim Foundation he briefly outlined his second book, and, as Perkins commented, nobody could expect a book to get written in such an extraordinary fashion. Poetry, a story with genuine unity, "no question of identification" of author and protagonist— all this he promised. But in promising it, he was trying to be the kind of writer he was not, and this blocked him for a time. As Elizabeth Nowell said, the core of the book was missing. Ignoring this, Wolfe wrote hundreds of pages of excellent material—paraphrases, introductions, discursions, which led him off in all directions. Perkins, who saw only selections, compared his own task with that of a man trying to hang on to the fin of a plunging whale.

Wolfe later described the genesis of *Of Time and the River* in *The Story of a Novel*. But, as Elizabeth Nowell has pointed out, the basic truth was simply that he had one story to tell—the story of Eugene Gant or George Webber or Thomas Wolfe. All attempts to avoid telling it led to blind alleys. So vast was his design that he could liken these chapters "to a row of lights which one sometimes sees at night from the windows of a speeding train, strung out across the dark and lonely countryside."[1]

At first Wolfe believed that this vast design could

be realized within the limits of one book, to be called "The October Fair." The manuscript, which lay long in the packing case, was never to appear in its original form. In later years Wolfe was to accuse Perkins of having harmed the manuscript by his vacillations. Perkins, for his part, was afraid that Aline Bernstein, might make difficulties or even bring charges. It took a while before Wolfe realized that he was working on a story that spanned almost a hundred and fifty years of American history, told through innumerable characters from all levels of society. This realization had dawned upon him as he wrote. He knew that "nevermore until death put its total and conclusive darkness on my life could I escape."[2]

In December 1933, after watching this excruciating process with silent anxiety, Perkins reached a decision. He calmly told Wolfe that his manuscript was finished. Wolfe looked at him in stunned surprise, then said that he was mistaken. The book was not finished; it could never be completed; he could write no more. Perkins insisted and told him to spend the next week in collecting in its proper order the manuscript that had been accumulated during the last two years. In 1942 Perkins revealed how urgently Wolfe had implored his help and how desperate he had been. And Perkins stood by him, professing a confidence he did not entirely feel, never hurrying the writer, showing him great consideration. Perhaps the book really was finished. As Wolfe saw it, however, it was really not a book so much as the skeleton of a book, but for the first time in four years the skeleton was all there.

Together they began to edit it, and Wolfe was filled with new hope and "a giant energy." Perkins distinguished two separate narratives, the first dealing with a man's youthful vagabondage and hunger for life, the second with a period of greater sureness, dominated by the unity of a single passion. The second narrative, which was to be included in *The Web and the Rock*, was much more complete than the first, which should logically have been finished and published first because in it is contained the substance of the years in Wolfe's life before he met Aline Bernstein. Wolfe worked indefatigably, and the first narrative was completed early in 1935. "I wrote too much again. I not only wrote what was essential, but time and time again my enthusiasm for a good scene would overpower me."[3] Perkins finally sent the manuscript to the printer while Wolfe was away on vacation. Had Wolfe been there he would certainly have insisted on further changes and amplifications. Wolfe later reproached Perkins for what he called his impatience and took strong exception to certain details.

And so the second novel was born. Chronologically *Of Time and the River: A Legend of Man's Hunger in His Youth* can be seen as a continuation of *Look Homeward, Angel*. No one would suspect from the simple, clear sequence that while he was writing it Wolfe felt like a drowning man. And so a book about America was born—or as much of America as could be encompassed in one superhuman effort. In terms of Wolfe's own life, *Of Time and the River* begins with his departure for Harvard (in 1920) and ends with his return from his first trip to Europe and his meeting with Aline Bernstein on the ship to America (1925). Wolfe's promise had not been exaggerated:

Through it all is poetry—the enormous rivers of the nation drinking the earth away at night, the vast rich stammer of night time in America, the lights, the smells, the thunder of the train—the savage summers, the fierce winters, the floods, the blizzards—all, all! And finally the great soft galloping of the horses of sleep![4]

To treat all problems of time in a meaningful way, to trace events backward through time was a difficult task. "I am haunted by a sense of time and a memory of things past and, of course, I know I have got to try somehow to get a harness on it."[5] Wolfe was a great rememberer. His memory was a storehouse where people, colors, sounds, the shading of a leaf, the unique line of a mouth were preserved forever. To discover a bed for the stream of recollections—this was the heart of his problem. By his ability to solve it, he would stand or fall as a writer. He distinguished present time, in which the story unfolds, from past time, in which the characters had lived their previous experiences.

Another major element was unchangeable, universal time, the time of the rivers, the mountains, the oceans, and the earth, which was to be contrasted with the bitter briefness of man's days. Though temperamentally quite different from Proust, and following a different system, he wanted to tell all about everything. "Pure time" would have impeded his passionate quest for the golden fleece of truth. As Günther Blöcker said, "his gift of memory is as direct, as sensuously naive, as

his universalism. Basically, he is as far from Proust as
he is from Joyce."

Man's greatness and frailty, his pride and humility
are imposed upon him by his transitoriness. While he
was working on this book, Wolfe read and reread Ec-
clesiastes and The Song of Songs, which, he said,
"make the narrative style of any modern novelist look
puny." The title "Of Time and the River" signifies the
working of time, memory and change, transience.

Wolfe's ears were alert to everything the stream of
time had to tell him—through distracted old Uncle
Bascom, through the French countess intent on gaining
the ear of an American journalist, through the kindly,
drunken doctor, through the voices of night and the
New York waterfront, and through his mother's endless
stories.

The young Eugene Gant is inhibited by the rejection and cool friendliness he encounters, just as the
feeling of not being understood had forced him to iso-
late himself behind his "wall" when he was a boy. The
world of rich Hudson River people, whom he meets
through a college acquaintance, deprives him of the
power of speech, the power to reveal in his own language the secrets of the big city and its people with
their diverse backgrounds. We see this in his conversation with Mrs. Pierce, the mother of that college acquaintance. (In real life the model of young Pierce was
Olin Dows, who painted a portrait of Wolfe as a young
man.) Insecure and inhibited as he was, Wolfe saw and
recognized for what they were the flickering shadows on
the wall, the "Circean make-believe—that world of

moonlight, magic and painted smoke that 'the river people' knew."[6]

Wolfe had an unusual instinct for summing up moments and recognizing decisive ones, much as some invisible antenna enables a connoisseur to date an undated painting. In a sudden blinding flash of recognition and horror he saw life transformed, saw the life-stifling dust of too much civilization, the rusty color of materialism. The subtitle, "A Legend of Man's Hunger in His Youth," also signifies growing insight that leads beyond suffering and greed as it grows. Eugene realizes that goodness and truth are "inextricably meshed, inwrought, and interwoven in that great web of horror, pain and sweat and bitter anguish, that great woven fabric of blind cruelty, hatred, filth and lust and tyranny and injustice, of joy, of faith, of love, of courage and devotion—that makes up life, and that resumes the world."[7]

All the sins and shortcomings that Wolfe can be accused of were brought up in an article entitled "Genius Is Not Enough" by the critic Bernard de Voto in the *Saturday Review of Literature* in 1936. There are writers like Hemingway who invariably write impeccably. And there are writers like Wolfe who need the help of a friend and editor in organizing, sorting out and assembling their material. Their compulsion to say everything prevents them from exercising firm control. In a letter to his friend Scott Fitzgerald, Wolfe came to the defense of "the great putter-inners," for whom there is just as much to be said as for the "taker-outers" like Monsieur Flaubert.[8] This was Wolfe's strength—as

well as the flaw in his strength. Perkins once divided
readers into two classes: those who have a good sense
of poetry and those who have a sense of the mystery of
life.

The critic Maxwell Geismar thinks that the six
years between *Look Homeward, Angel* and *Of Time
and the River*, the years from 1929 to 1935, were the
most interesting years in Wolfe's career, the years in
which he progressed from an apprentice to a craftsman,
from revolt to "realization," insight, and certainty.
(The fruit of awakening, so to speak, is seen most
clearly in *You Can't Go Home Again,* as I shall point
out in a later chapter.) Geismar calls *Of Time and the
River* Wolfe's best book because of its sharpened perspective and brilliant descriptions of these various
spheres of experience. An episode such as the one of
Starwick in Europe—probably the best single passage
in the whole work—is an example of the kind of mastery that went into hundreds of scenes, creating the vast
panorama of this world.

With this book Wolfe cleared the difficult, fright-
ening hurdle of the second novel. He was in Berlin in
1935 when the favorable verdict of the American press
reached him. In *Uns bleibt die Erde* Heinz Ledig-
Rowohlt, a German friend of Wolfe's, describes the
scene: Wolfe, a beaming giant with a shock of wild
black hair, standing in a little artists' cafe in the Kleist-
strasse, shouting: "Let's all have some wine. I'm rich!"
In fact he never was rich. But his second great venture
had succeeded.

His elation over the reception of *Of Time and the*

River, however, was short-lived. A few months after publication he was at the brink of despair, rage, and madness. Lawsuits in several different states brought by literary agents and by a Brooklyn family that claimed that it had been libeled in the story "No Door" took their toll in money, time, and health. Hallucinations and nightmares disturbed his sleep and exhausted his feverish, overstrained mind. His advance of three thousand dollars from Scribner's was spent, and he still owed income tax on it. No money was coming in. He quarreled with Perkins, and the ensuing estrangement from him and from Scribner's drove him into a state of exhaustion and dangerous irritability.

In Paris in 1936 he could not sleep and feared that he was going mad, because "all unity and control of personality seemed to have escaped from me."[9] Bad moods or disagreeable conditions that prevented him from working always produced great inner tension and strained relations with others. Nevertheless, he came through this great crisis unharmed. The lawsuits were settled favorably, though the costs were high. Later, matured and reconciled, Wolfe could look back on them with wry humor. He felt a renewed desire to work and gained important insights in his search for truth. In a letter to Arthur Mann, the sportswriter, he jokingly remarked that "the late Charles Dickens by no means exhausted the subject of law and justice in his observations of the law and on the courts—I think we could teach him a few new tricks nowadays that would make him rub his eyes."[10]

In 1936, the year of the Olympic Games, he made

his last visit to Europe, to Germany, the country of the
thinkers and writers he had loved and admired as a
student. While Wolfe was in love with America, he
always felt drawn to Europe. He thought highly of the
English and the Germans, although he was not blind to
their weaknesses. On that last trip he sensed the im-
pending disaster, which he did not live to see. "I felt all
summer that it might be the last time I saw Europe
before another great war breaks out," he wrote to his
mother.

With a bystander's detachment Wolfe recognized
the true state of affairs:

It is hard to see how they are going to keep out of [a war]. They
are building up tremendous armies everywhere. . . . The air is
full of bitterness and hatred toward each other. Germany is a
wonderful country and the Germans are great people, but it
looks as if, under this present regime, they are heading for war.[11]

In 1937 Wolfe's long article on Germany entitled
"I Have a Thing to Tell You" was to be published.
Despite his great sympathy for that country and its
people, he had decided that truth demanded its publication. He did not mince his words in describing conditions in Germany and spoke his mind about Hitler, the
"dark Messiah." At its appearance Heinz Ledig-
Rowohlt was justifiably concerned for his own safety in
fascist Germany. Wolfe had been the guest of both the
Rowohlts, father and son. Connoisseurs of literature,
they entertained him royally, making him feel "as
happy as King Tamberlane."

In October 1936 he wrote confidentially to his old

college friend Jonathan Daniels that he was back at work, that it was "all coming with a rush," and that for the past several weeks he had been writing more than five thousand words a day. In the early summer of 1937 he wrote six short stories in eight weeks. Among them were some that he revised to become important sections of *You Can't Go Home Again*. He also thought seriously of combining the social satire "The Party at Jack's" and a few other pieces into a self-contained book whose action "would occur within the limits of a single twenty-four hours." This idea, however, was dropped. Instead, he wrote the pages that would become *You Can't Go Home Again*, a decisive concluding chapter of the "master book," dealing with the end of the protagonist's love for Esther and his visit to his home in the "city of lost men." It contains descriptions of the horrors of the big city, the portrait of Lloyd McHarg (modeled on Sinclair Lewis), the 1936 visit to Germany, and the break with the protagonist's friend and editor, Foxhall Edwards.

4

The Last Years

Two more books completed by Wolfe himself appeared during his lifetime: the "progress report" entitled *The Story of a Novel* (1936) and *From Death to Morning* (1935), a collection of short stories including one called "The Web of Earth," which Perkins and most of the critics rated very highly. The title "From Death to Morning" implies that the writer, wandering about the city at night, a prey to anguish and despair, is close to death when the light of morning liberates him and shows him the way to pursue in his quest for truth.

How is the estrangement from Max Perkins, that great editor, friend, and lover of literature, to be explained? It was a long, complicated affair. Elizabeth Nowell, who enjoyed Wolfe's full confidence, both as his literary agent and as a personal friend and adviser, said laconically that there was no law requiring anyone to stay with his first publisher for life, especially if he felt that to do so would be harmful to his reputation or to his creative talent. The allegations of obtuse critics that Wolfe could never have published his work without the help of his editor must have been just as distressing to the sensitive writer as their constant harping on the autobiographical nature of the work. Wolfe had gained self-confidence over the years. He had outgrown the phase when he needed a father figure to help him cope with the difficulties of life. Yet none of this adequately explains his desperate decision to break with Perkins. They were too deeply bound by friendship and by the respect of one great man for another. Wolfe could not deny how much Perkins (the great figure of Foxhall Edwards in the posthumous *You Can't Go Home*

Again) had done for him—nor did he wish to. There is no doubt, however, that Perkins was far more conservative than Wolfe in his views about the social system, social relations, and people.

When Wolfe told Perkins that to him living meant writing and overcoming death, he meant it literally. He wasn't going to make even the smallest concession for the sake of personal or social obligations. "Like Mr. Joyce, I am going to write as I please, and this time, no one is going to cut me unless I want them to. . . . Like Mr. Joyce, I have at last discovered my own America, I believe I have found my language, I think I know my way."[1]

The letter from which this quotation is taken covers twenty printed pages. Wolfe wrote it on 15 December 1936 but did not mail it until 10 January 1937—after much cogitation. Perkins was a conservative man; Wolfe was afraid that his own natural impulse of creation might "be killed at its inception by cold caution, by indifference, by the growing apprehensiveness and dogmatism of your own conservatism."[2] Perkins was uneasy about Wolfe's radical political views, which they had discussed when he was working on *Of Time and the River*. He was also worried that Wolfe might write about the people at Scribner's. Wolfe had to pursue his own vision of the world and society. He did not belong to any of the cliques or groups of the early 1930s when America was in the morass of the great depression. He rightly pointed out to Perkins that he could not be called a radical. "You know that my whole feeling toward life could not be indicated or included under such

a category. I am not a party man, I am not a propaganda man, I am not a Union Square or Greenwich
Village communist. . . . I not only do not believe in
these people: I do not even believe they believe in
themselves."[3]

Firm convictions clashed with equally firm ones.
But their differences were not the decisive issue. Wolfe
felt that what was at stake was his whole life, the
strength and creativity he needed to write and publish a
new book. After all, no major work by him had appeared since 1935, though the second narrative in "The
October Fair" had been drafted by 1933.

Desperately brooding and intent upon bringing the
matter to a head, Wolfe sent Perkins a telegram from
New Orleans on 9 January 1937 asking: "What is your
offer?" Perkins sent him a noncommittal reply. Why he
hesitated to give Wolfe a direct yes or no answer is not
clear. Elizabeth Nowell says that Scribner's may never
have made Wolfe a definite offer because Perkins understood that Wolfe wanted to break with them for
deeply rooted and complex reasons and that the sev-
erance was inevitable. Here the judicious Miss Nowell
may be arguing too subtly. Even if Perkins felt the
break to be inevitable, he was still under an obligation
to make a contractual offer. Whatever his reasons, he
did not do so. Wolfe's decision was neither a betrayal
nor a whim. As he wrote to Sherwood Anderson in
September 1937: "It maddens me not to get published:
I feel at times like getting every publisher in the world
by the scruff of his neck, forcing his jaws open, and
cramming the manuscript down his throat—'God damn
you, here it is—I will and must be published.' "[4]

Was it vanity or desire for fame? What was preying on Wolfe's mind and threatening his sanity was something far more serious than that. What he was begging for was "the merciful damned easement of oblivion" that comes when a book is published, when "for good or ill, for better or for worse—it's over, done with, finished, out of your life forever."[5] Perkins assured Wolfe that he was ready to help him if he could, whenever he needed it.

This was true, but it was also true that Wolfe's manuscripts were not being published, and this made him struggle blindly like a whale fighting for its life. When he told Sherwood Anderson that not being published maddened him, he was speaking literally. "This has been almost like death," he said. "But I *will* be published, if I can: I've got to be—and I will have my own picture of life, my own vision of society."[6] After endless quarreling and letters, the friends parted—but not irrevocably. In February 1938 Perkins voluntarily testified on Wolfe's behalf in a lawsuit.

In the late summer of 1937 Wolfe asked several publishing houses whether they might be interested in publishing his manuscripts. He did this by telephone; some of the editors were not even sure that it was Wolfe himself they were speaking to. Depressed as he was, Wolfe was incapable of more effective action. He corresponded with Robert N. Linscott, who had written to him on the basis of word from the publishing grapevine. Wolfe liked this sympathetic older man and began to discuss the publication of the second narrative of "The October Fair."

Linscott acknowledged receipt of "one packing

case and nine packages of manuscripts" and scrupulously advised the writer that he had no fireproof safe and that Wolfe would have to assume the risk. Wolfe was upset at what he interpreted as an attempt to take advantage of him and wrote a stiff letter to Linscott, which he never mailed. The preliminary negotiations ended. In all the years Wolfe had been with Scribner's they had never brought up the question of responsibility for his manuscripts—and the chronic fear of victimization this would have aroused in him. In December he finally signed a contract with Harper & Brothers and began his association with his new editor, Edward C. Aswell.

After these trying months Wolfe agreed to give a talk on his working methods to the students of Purdue University, Indiana, in May 1938. Before his trip he worked day and night, assembling his manuscript so that the publishers could get an idea of it. He hoped he would be able to complete the rewriting, additions, and revisions and have the manuscript ready for the printer in about a year, provided he could work on it undisturbed when he returned from his lecture trip and vacation. He told his mother he expected to be back in New York City in June. After the excitement and drudgery of the past year he wanted to relax a little on the trip and take the luxury train—this lover of railroads and mysterious transience, who discerned in the "tremendous and nameless Allness of The Station . . . not lives but life, . . . the vast murmur of these voices drowsily caught up there like the murmurous and incessant sound of time and of eternity, which is and is forever, no matter what men come and go through the portals of the great Station, no matter what men live or die."[7]

During the trip he visited some of his mother's relatives, descendants of old Bacchus Westall. He wanted to see his cousins again, "to get the whole history of the Pentlands out West for a future book." He enjoyed the pause between periods of hard work, but he could not rest. A jaunt undertaken on the spur of the moment turned into a deadly test of endurance: with two journalists, he set out on a marathon car trip. They toured the whole West, covering 3,300 miles in eight days—"in other words a complete swing around the West from the Rocky Mountains on, and every big national park in the West." Wolfe abandoned his plan to leave his companions in Spokane and return directly to New York City. In spite of the exertion he was in excellent spirits. "When I get through, I shall really have seen America (except Texas)," he wrote to Elizabeth Nowell, while on this "furious, hectic, crowded and wildly comical" expedition.

He estimated that the notebooks he had exuberantly filled contained thirty thousand words. (As usual, he overestimated. His suitcase contained notes amounting to about 11,400 words—"the whole thing smacked down with the blinding speed and variety of the trip." This journal was published in 1951 under the title *A Western Journal.*) He was pleased with himself; the notes meant a lot to him. "I really feel ready to go again. . . . I *wanted* to write them—couldn't keep from it," he told Elizabeth Nowell.[8]

He arrived in Vancouver after this marathon seriously ill, shivering with a high fever and complaining that it hurt him to breathe. On the boat trip to Victoria and Vancouver he had shared a bottle of whisky with a "poor, shivering wretch" from whom he may have contracted a respiratory infection. Instead of going to a hospital, he returned to Seattle, where he stayed for five days at a hotel, seriously ill. A friend, James Stevens, called his own physician, Dr. E. C. Ruge, an unusually sound diagnostician, who recognized the illness as pneumonia and had him admitted to a hospital. On 15 July Wolfe sent Aswell a telegram saying that the doctors now considered him out of danger. But complications arose, and chest X-rays disclosed a shadow from an old tubercular lesion. Wolfe was still suffering from terrible headaches and temporary lapses of consciousness. His sister Mabel came to Seattle and with the help of a nurse took him by train across the continent to Baltimore. On the way the headaches sometimes became unbearable, and Wolfe was subject to additional spells of irrationality.

At Johns Hopkins Hospital in Baltimore, Dr. Walter E. Dandy obtained his permission for an exploratory brain operation to confirm the tentative diagnosis of a more or less benign tumor. The headaches temporarily abated, and Wolfe jubilantly told Aswell that "they'd fixed it" and took heart. Though there was now little hope, the doctors proposed a major operation. Wolfe's family and friends watched as he was wheeled away down the hospital corridor. Perkins was there but did not see him because he did not want to take the risk of exciting him. Finding tubercles in the brain, Dr. Dandy abandoned the operation. Three days later, on the morning of 15 September 1938, Wolfe died without having spoken another fully conscious word.

His posthumous work reinforced and heightened his literary reputation. The tremendous task of sorting out, assembling, and publishing Wolfe's papers fell to Edward C. Aswell.

5

The Web
and the
Rock

It is about one man's discovery
of life and of the world,
and in this sense it is a book
of apprenticeship.[1]

The Web and the Rock, posthumously published in 1939, with many of its sections still unfinished, reveals a new way of thinking. Toward the end of his life Wolfe was moving away from his old plans and ideas. But given the way he wrote, this did not mean a change of subject matter. After his years of wandering, he was ready to fit the experience of love into a new, vaster context, integrating and subordinating it. By the time of his death he had lost interest in the second narrative of his old manuscript, "The October Fair," and was no longer upset by his publisher's delay in bringing it out. He was in the process of establishing new values. His hero was no longer to be called Spangler or—satirically —Joe Doaks. Wolfe had become a great admirer of Tolstoy. Influenced by Goethe, he was also thinking of creating an American Wilhelm Meister.

Not revolt but a new awareness filled his mind. Through George Webber (as he finally named his American Wilhelm Meister) he was building bridges toward the outside world and his fellow men. He was through with self-justification. While his protagonist had to be a person in his own right, his significance was to lie "not in his personal uniqueness and differences, but in his personal identity to the life of every man,"[2] that is, a character that encompasses every man. The "realization" aroused a feeling of belonging that Wolfe had never known before. It also meant that he was drawing away from the rebellion of his youth and from his years of wandering. "In other words, the value of the Eugene Gant type is his personal and romantic uniqueness, causing conflict with the world around him: in this sense, the Eugene Gant type of character becomes a kind of romantic self-justification, and the greatest weakness of the Eugene Gant type of character lies in this fact."[3]

New problems, some of them technical, now confronted him. He was so carried away by the significance and impact of his "realization" that he thrust Eugene Gant aside with unwarranted violence and replaced him with George Webber. For his own reasons he changed his protagonist's name and his childhood as well as outward appearance. Instead of being six feet, six inches tall, Webber is conspicuous because of his unusually long arms. Wolfe was indeed trying not to be autobiographical in any literal sense.

One major reason for the emergence of George Webber may have been, as Günther Blöcker and John Hall Wheelock claim, that Wolfe chose this approach in reaction to the criticism of writing autobiographical novels. Aswell, however, pointed out that Wolfe still had many important things to say about his childhood he had omitted from *Look Homeward, Angel*, and that the only way to say them was through a new character. "He wanted a new name to hang out like a flag, proclaiming his emancipation from his former self."[4]

Perkins later wrote that "it was a horrible crime that he should have departed from his inevitable scheme by trying to change his mother into an aunt and himself, who had been Eugene, into George Webber."[5]

The question remains: Was Wolfe wise to forego Eugene Gant? Was Aswell right in believing that Wolfe needed a new protagonist in order to write again about his childhood and youth? Or was Perkins right in considering this departure a mistake? (Perkins later saw the matter in perspective: the name Webber was neither a better nor a worse mask for Wolfe than the name Gant.) Was Maxwell Geismar right when he wrote that Wolfe was wise in deciding to go back and develop a new version of his protagonist's youth and education in keeping with Wolfe's own new values?

There is no reason, however, why Eugene Gant, as he gained experience of life, could not plausibly have changed course, undergone a transformation, found a new vision, just as did the man he represented: Thomas Wolfe. I find Wolfe's first version of his past better and more authentic. Biographical retouching is like copying a painting. The reversion again diverted Wolfe unnecessarily from the chronicle of his life and times. If "The October Fair" had been published as written, Wolfe's writing might well have taken a different course. Perkins expressed no opinion on that.

But it is useless to speculate. Aswell had to decide how best to prepare the work for publication; the manuscript had not been finally assembled.

Following his plan of writing more or less simultaneously over the full spread of his chronicle, Tom had thought and worked his way along to the end of *You Can't Go Home Again*. Whether he saw that as a separate volume I cannot say. He really thought of the entire George Webber story as "The Web and the Rock," with the different parts of it carrying their own subheadings. The first subheading was "The Hills Beyond," another repeated the general title, the last was "You Can't Go Home Again."[6]

Several passages in Wolfe's letters confirm this comment.

Aswell has described how he went about this almost impossible task. As Aswell noted, it falls into two separate halves: George's childhood and apprenticeship, and the love story that Wolfe previously intended to publish as "The October Fair." The first part is written in the later, more restrained style appropriate to the ideas and plans inspired by Wolfe's "realization." Wolfe never got around to rewriting the love story, though he went through it, made some changes, and rewrote a few passages. The disparity between the two halves of the book unmistakably reveals the shift in his thinking and can be seen in the two different styles. As Aswell regretfully pointed out, the two halves failed to join properly.

The first part of *The Web and the Rock* represents a transition to *You Can't Go Home Again*. As Floyd C. Watkins has shown in such cogent detail in *Thomas Wolfe's Characters* (1957), Wolfe imposed many limitations on himself in his effort to avoid repetition. For Wolfe it was much more difficult to create an only child raised by a puritanical old aunt, as he did in George Webber, than to describe a boy growing up in a big family like the Gants, together with brothers, sisters, and neighbors. Perspectives and undertones clearly indicate the development of George's social conscience,

creating the background for George's growth toward
maturity, as Wolfe outlined it with such flair and enthusiasm in his letters. For all the sharpness of detail,
Altamont (Asheville) in *Look Homeward, Angel* was
shown in a somewhat poetic, romantic light. Through
Libya Hill, Wolfe was already setting the stage for the
social criticism that would come to the fore in his last
book, *You Can't Go Home Again.* Impoverished, de-
generate mountain folk who have migrated to Libya
Hill or its outskirts; the plight of the powerless classes;
the way in which slum life destroys human dignity—
these were subjects that were not dealt with in *Look
Homeward, Angel.*

Watkins attributes the different ambience of these
two fictional accounts of Wolfe's youth to Wolfe's development of two different protagonists. While Eugene
is always a vital part of his environment, 'Monk'
Webber (as he is nicknamed on account of his appearance) is more of an outsider. He sees a lot but plays a
less active role.

Out of stories, memories, and episodes Wolfe cre-
ates a colorful, dynamic, multi-level picture of a small
town. He introduces some sixty new characters, but the
Gants and the breath of passion that marks *Look
Homeward, Angel* are missing. College days (this time
in Pine Rock), George's life in New York City as a
budding writer, and his application for a teaching position at the "School for Utility Cultures" are treated less
exhaustively than in *Look Homeward, Angel* and *Of
Time and the River.* Certain sections or chapters such
as "The Butcher," "The Child by Tiger," and "The

Priestly One" are still very close to the world of "Gant-ism." This greatly enhances the narrative interest. The much admired chapter entitled "The Child by Tiger" deals with the unseen psychological depths that under-lie the mysterious ferment of the South.

The love story between George Webber and Esther Jack belongs entirely to the context of *Of Time and the River*. In fact, it is quite conceivable that some-day it may be assigned to a more appropriate place in the total framework of Wolfe's work. If Wolfe, that insatiable reviser, had lived long enough to get *The Web and the Rock* into final shape, much would have been changed. Since he was not able to do so, the mov-ing love story remains essentially as he first wrote it. In one way this is fortunate, since the mature Wolfe, hav-ing outgrown Gantism, would probably have painted over and dimmed the original colors. But it is also re-grettable, because he would probably—and quite rightly—have cut out many repetitious and tedious pas-sages. Whatever we may think of Eugene-George, alias Thomas Wolfe, the story in its extant form describes a joyous yet distressing and difficult period in the lives of an intelligent, warm-hearted woman and a distrusting genius, twenty years younger than she, who is becoming more and more critical of his society and of wealth.

Wolfe the writer never spared Wolfe the man. He called ugly scenes ugly, and unfounded suspicions un-founded. Periods in which all of love's old warmth and tenderness are recaptured alternated with periods dark-ened by the desperate, ugly, bitter struggle between George and Esther. At such times George had "lost his squeal," his "wild goat-cry" of exuberance and the sheer joy of living. Without it life was no more than a listless vegetating.

Both the descriptions of the sweetness of love and of love's frenzies are based on experience:

When the convulsion of pain and horror drove him mad, he sought again the spurious remedy of the bottle . . . until he went out in the street to find the enemy, to curse and brawl and seek out death and hatred in dive and stew, among the swarms of the rats of the flesh, the livid, glittering dead men of the night.[7]

Perkins used to speak of Wolfe's dualism, and this dualism caused madness and infatuation, on the one hand, and sanity and confidence, on the other hand, to clash with the impact of surging armies. Then the specters of madness and death would leave him as suddenly as they had besieged him, "and he would come back in the morning, come back from death to morning, walking on the Bridge."[8]

Perkins had become familiar with those mercurial shifts, those walks that took Wolfe from death to morning, after the publication of *Look Homeward, Angel*. On the good days George knew how much Esther loved him. Why after all had she left the luxury and beauty of her home for the cyclonic chaos of his shabby home? Why did she lavish love and tenderness upon him, cook for him, put up with his moods, meet his self-doubt with faith, defend this difficult personality who was a genius? She gives him some of her life wisdom and strength. She tries, with her freshness and clear-sightedness, to drive away the specters of night and suspicion, to banish "the enemy."

What horror did you want to flee? Must you forever be a fool without a faith and eat your flesh?

"The horror of eight million faces!"

Remember eight—know one.

"The horror of two million books!"

Write one that has two thousand words of wisdom in it.

"Each window is a light, each light a room, each room a cell, each cell a person!"[9]

Esther teaches George to accept himself. And the author who wrote this regarded himself as a critical camera eye, as well as one painting enigmatically an objective self-portrait. He acknowledged that she had entered so deeply into him that he would never lose her again. Her intelligence and wisdom helped him to make his discoveries. "Is not a man, then, taller than a tower?" Thomas Wolfe the writer learned to distinguish madness from reality, to heighten his awareness of life by diminishing his awareness of self:

The world is a better place than I thought it was—for all its spots and smudges . . . a far, far better and more shining place! . . . nothing in life has turned out the way I expected . . . nothing is the way I thought it was going to be.[10]

Wolfe recognized that within this delicate form of Aline Bernstein lay invincible strength of will. He loved her and he left her. He went abroad to escape from her, but also to escape from his life in New York City.

The final section of *The Web and the Rock* bears the title of the abandoned book: "The October Fair." It marks a turning point, a summing up, and a new vision. It brings the chronicle of Wolfe's life up to a still fluid phase.

George reaches a crossroads. The direction he chooses is the direction Wolfe was trying to imply when he changed his protagonist's name. George "had got a little Wisdom for" himself. Like Wolfe, this Gant too, though his name is now Webber, has recognized and accepted his limitations. The final chapter of Book VII, "The Looking Glass," (presumably written relatively late) represents the harvest of Wolfe's pilgrimage in quest of truth and his artistic compulsion "to tell all about it." It is the summation of all that has happened, the permanent, indestructible treasure cast up by the river.

George used to look at himself in the glass—"but outside of it, and opposite." To use Harry Emerson Fosdick's metaphor, he was like a man who has been living in a mind that is like a room surrounded by mirrors. Every way he turned he saw himself. Then some of the mirrors changed to windows. This is what happened after the fight at the Munich Oktoberfest, as Ernst von Salomon's memoir recalls. The convalescent patient discovered that there was no escape route leading back to the past and that anyone who seeks one is lost, like Jim, the old sportsman and braggart in *The Web and the Rock*.

Wolfe wrote many letters about this transformation. One sentence describes its importance with aphoristic brevity: "I think my interests have increasingly turned away from the person writing the book toward the book the person is writing." The young Gant has grown older. As George Webber, he feels that "the spirit that dwelt behind this ruined mask now looked calmly and sanely forth upon the earth for the first time in ten years."[11] The past no longer overshadows the present. He can no longer take refuge in the caves of memory and time, though the images and voices of the past are not forgotten.

[It] was a good time then, for there were all the things that came and went, the steps, the basket, and the bright nasturtiums— . . .

And then Crane's cow again, and morning, morning in the thickets of the memory, and so many lives-and-deaths of life so long ago, . . . and all lost voices . . . of lost kinsmen in the mountains long ago. . . . That was a good time then.[12]

The past no longer beckons enticingly, because "you can't go home again."

In his foreword to *The Web and the Rock*, Wolfe again stressed that the novel contained invented characters, that he "sought a release of his inventive power." These assurances were a courteous rejoinder to the critics' charges of being autobiographical, but he had long ago grown beyond the range of their disparagements. The Wolfe reflected in the concluding pages of *The Web and the Rock* proves that his belief in his transformation was not self-deception but a true index to his thinking. "Now he looked at his body without falsehood or rancor, and with wonder that he dwelt there in this place. He knew and accepted now its limitations."[13] Wolfe had accepted his limits—thus extending them in all directions.

6

You Can't Go Home Again

The novel *You Can't Go Home Again* (1940) represents an impressive keystone in the arch so brilliantly begun with *Look Homeward, Angel*; it marks the high point of Wolfe's artistic experience and reflects the peak of his life experience. He insisted on writing these pages in defiance of all rules and conventions, even if this meant alienation and exile. "But whatever happens I shall write this book." He feared that death might take him before he had finished his work, and his fear was well founded. This was the second book Aswell pieced together out of a chest-high stack of manuscripts after Wolfe's death.

You Can't Go Home Again in its existing form is the most mature fruit of his "discovery," of his changed relationship to his fellow men and to society. Out of the sadness of the two last years of his life came the ironical sketches of upper-class follies and parrot talk about art, a symbolic skyscraper fire with sinister undertones just before the Wall Street crash of 1929, a scathing indictment of a mercenary society and of a ruthless business corporation. And out of that same sadness came Wolfe's statement of his final creed, a literary testament setting the seal upon his life and his ideas.

Wolfe had achieved an apparently effortless mastery of technique, maintaining narrative verve and rendering city slang faithfully. Günther Blöcker thinks *You Can't Go Home Again* is by far the best of Wolfe's posthumously published books. "The lyrical tremolo of his early works has quieted down into an objective narrative style without losing any of its youthful brio."[1]

This novel, which Aswell pieced together with the

help of transitional passages from Wolfe's letters, covers the period from Wolfe's return from Europe in 1930 up to his last trip to Germany in 1936 and the break with Perkins soon after. Looking backward at his themes, from *Look Homeward, Angel* to *The Hills Beyond*, one sees that his themes reflect almost all his problems. The path Wolfe had taken was that of a small-town boy freeing himself from his conservative background and becoming a student, that of a playwright becoming a novelist, a critic of his times, and a moralist.

In *You Can't Go Home Again* Wolfe realized the great plan that his new insights had inspired. He was so excited by the broadening of his horizons that an entire book about the love of a man and woman and about being young in a huge city now began to seem "subordinate to the whole plan of the book he had in mind." In this great part of a great work he successfully drew the conclusions of his "realization," stated his views, and wrote his most objective and, by the same token, most autobiographical book. He wanted to be objective yet autobiographical in a special sense. Instead of being caught up in self-centered conflicts, his protagonist was to be a figure that would bring to light universal and eternal truths. He was to be like a pebble thrown into a pool. Wolfe threw his Wilhelm Meister pebble into the pool, thus touching off a whole series of concentric circles. The pebble was only a means to an end, not the center in the Gantian sense. "The most important thing is to tell about the thing itself, the thing that happens. The pebble, if you like, is only a means to this end."[2]

Wolfe's programmatic and technical analysis of the pebble metaphor is theory—a rational theory nourished by experience and anguish. But the pages of *You Can't Go Home Again* are art, or, as Faulkner said in his generous tribute to Wolfe, an attempt to engrave all the experience of the human heart on a pinhead. He wanted to describe a new life-consciousness, as Goethe, Swift, and Tolstoy had done. Ever since his early playwriting days, he had been perfecting his artistry to serve this tremendous plan. "Mr. Perkins," he had written in 1930, "no one has ever written a book about America —no one has ever put into it the things I know and the things everyone knows."[3] Perkins was aware of the size of the territory his friend was staking out. "To reveal America and Americans to Americans. That was at the heart of Tom's fierce life."

For Wolfe satirical exaggeration was an essential part of life, particularly American life. "No man . . . who wants to write a book about America on a grand scale can hardly escape feeling again and again the emotion of the man when he first saw a giraffe: 'I don't believe it!' "[4]

In the chapter of *You Can't Go Home Again* entitled "The Party at Jack's" Wolfe wrote a harsh but momentous sentence. Describing an uninhibited young woman whose wealth still could not buy what she was probably looking for, he said: "She had tried everything in life—except living." Amy Carleton, famous for her girlish beauty, her elflike face and ebony curls, surpassed the ultimate limits of notoriety, even for New York City. Despite her beauty, charm, and intelligence, she lacked the will, the toughness, to resist. In being subject to a feverish tempo heightened to insane excess she was the child of her time. She had been everywhere and seen everything—"in the way one might see things from the windows of an express train traveling eighty miles an hour." One might meet her in New York City, "a freckled, laughing image of happy innocence," and within ten days "come upon her again in the corruptest gatherings of Paris, drugged fathoms deep in opium, foul-bodied and filth-bespattered, cloying in the embraces of a gutter rat, so deeply rooted in the cesspool that it seemed she must have been bred on sewage and had never known any other life."[5] She had lost the way, so there was nothing left for her to do but die.

For Wolfe, to squander life was to betray its enigmatic, particular quality. Among his discoveries was the realization that to try to escape from the world is a confession of great weakness. This is what he meant by the warning "you can't go home again." There is no way back to family or childhood, to romantic love or youthful dreams of fame and honor. There is no returning to a long-sought-for father or to anyone who might bear one's burden, no way back to old forms and systems that in reality are constantly changing. The only thing to do is to resist weakness and evil and the easy way out, and to overcome the enemy—an enemy "as old as time and evil as Hell."

Wolfe feared death as his enemy, but death taught him to know more about life, to perceive its special quality. Unlike the giddy society ladies and demimondaines, the unidentified man in the chapter entitled

"The Hollow Men" rebels against being nothing but a "poor, shabby and corrupted cipher" and jumps from a hotel window rather than live on as a nameless atom. The hotel is called the Admiral Drake, and Wolfe harangues the admiral, refuting the ideas of "the hollow men" and contrasting the dignity of death with debased and lost life.

The figure of girlish, corrupt Amy Carleton typifies the confusing, complex interweaving of portrait and model, of straight autobiography and literary adaptation. The protagonist is the pebble that Wolfe drops into the pool to make the concentric circles through which he will describe relationships. The connection between truth and fiction is singularly complicated. The sound criticism demonstrated in the novels carries over into the personal correspondence—and vice versa.

In June 1935 Wolfe wrote a few lines (which he never mailed) to Aline Bernstein from Copenhagen, telling her that he had read in the paper that a friend of hers, a Mrs. Whitfield, had shot herself. Whether or not this Mrs. Whitfield was the model for Amy Carleton is irrelevant. The point is that by means of Amy Carleton Wolfe was passing judgment on a certain segment of society and condemning its way of life. His bitter verdict on the Jacks and their friends recurs throughout the letters, succinctly stated, without novelistic subtlety or the colorful, characteristic style of his fiction. "It was a lie of life, false, cynical, scornful, drunk with imagined power, and rotten to the core."[6] In the great jungle of the city he saw "acts of sickening violence and cruelty in a cruel and corrupt authority, trampling ruthlessly below its feet the lives of the poor, the weak, the wretched, and defenseless of the earth."[7]

Amid the extravagant profusion of scenes, Chapter 8 of *You Can't Go Home Again*, which bears the simple title of "The Company," stands out as a masterpiece of critical satire. The "immensely agreeable" Mr. Merrit, always ready with a joke, his pockets full of savory cigars that he hands out on the slightest provocation, is a "company man," but he is also a diabolical agent masquerading as a benevolent traveling man. He, no less than the crowd of shivering derelicts huddling at night in the underground public latrines of New York City, reveals to George Webber the brutality of human behavior. The hand that jokes, slaps shoulders, shakes other hands, becomes a ghastly paw, pounding the table in the little office. The jovial voice has a ring of primordial evil as Mr. Merrit tells Webber's troubled friend Randy Shepperton that the Company has lost confidence in him and that unless his quota improves he is through. "You get the business or out you go."

This demon is only a menial in the hierarchy of the Company. At the top stood "if not God himself, then the next thing to it"—Mr. Paul S. Appleton III, otherwise known as P.S.A. Every year at the annual salesmen's meeting Mr. Appleton would stand in front of a map of the United States and make an impassioned speech of prophetic exhortation. "There's your market! Go out and sell them!" Through the writer's mind flashed a terrible picture of a great pharaoh applying a thonged whip to the naked back of his chief overseer, who in turn was whipping the man in front of him, and

so on down the line. The satirical account closes with
the laconic remark that George Webber "had just found
out something about life that he had not known before."

Like most of Wolfe's scenes, this chapter about
the almighty Company has its corresponding links with
reality. Writing to Margaret Roberts, with whom he
was now reconciled, about his new book and about his
sister Mabel and her husband (whom he had already
portrayed as Hugh Barton and who appears in the
Webber cycle as Randy Shepperton), Tom told her that
he felt like a social outcast. "My whole spirit and feeling is irresistibly on the side of the working class,
against the cruelty, the injustice, the corrupt and in-
famous privilege of great wealth, against the shocking
excess and wrong of the present system." The artist
who makes his art the vehicle for political dogma and
intolerant propaganda is a lost man. Nevertheless "I
think almost every great poet and every great writer
who ever wrote and whose works we all love and treasure has been on the side of the oppressed, the suffering,
the confused and lost and stricken of the earth."

Wolfe castigates his brother-in-law's employers for
"kicking him out ruthlessly, brutally and without no-
tice" after thirty years of service. While he concedes
that the firm had the right to dismiss the elderly man,
because he had been paid in exchange for his services,
he still says: "to hell with all such reasoning; it is probably in accord with the ruthless code of business proce-
dure, but it is not in accord with human life, with
human justice, with human decency."[8]

Wolfe voted for Franklin D. Roosevelt for president in 1932, after Herbert Hoover's terrible failure in
office. He recognized the stupidity of the great depression's being characterized by so-called experts as "a
swing of the pendulum." By 1931 it was clear to him
that the governmental and economic crisis would never
be solved by old methods and outdated expedients.
Wolfe commented sardonically:

Meanwhile, Mr. Hoover ("The Great Engineer," you know) and
the other noble politicians are giving a wonderful illustration of
the blind man searching in a dark room for a black cat that isn't
there. There are seven million out of work—and Mr. Hoover
issues a call for $20,000,000 so that each of the unemployed will
have $2.50 to squander away during the winter.[9]

Wolfe later became critical of President Roosevelt
too, although he supported him for reelection in 1936.
Though he saw many of the Roosevelt administration
measures as appalling errors, he felt that:

. . . the worst calamity that could happen [to] this country at the
present time would be the election of a reactionary government,
and . . . this present administration, whatever its errors of com-
mission or omission may have been, has made the only decisive
movement that has been made in the direction of social progress
and social justice since the administration of Woodrow Wilson.[10]

In *You Can't Go Home Again* Wolfe told the
story of the feverish speculation of the boom and the
catastrophe of the great depression in his own way,
through a setting he knew thoroughly: his home town.
The real-estate speculators pursue their business like
mad, infecting one another with their insanity. Within a
short time, in an intoxication of waste and wild destruc-

tiveness, the whole face of the town is changed. Wolfe
reiterated the theme of *Welcome to Our City*—big talk
and expansive gestures. ("Within a few years Libya
Hill is going to be the largest and most beautiful city in
the state. You mark my words."[11]) Selling and buying
back is the game of the day. The speculators ruthlessly
exploit their town, ruining their children and their children's children. The failure of the Libya Hill bank ex-
poses a deep inner collapse. To the guilty gamblers
blind Judge Bland (a freely invented character) seems
like one delegated by the Eumenides to punish the sin-
ful.

America in the fall of 1929 seemed to be both at
an end and at a beginning. Looking back, he accused
Americans of having become a nation of advertising
men, victims of catchwords like "prosperity" and "the
American way"—charges he had already made in his
student days.

In the following years Wolfe was to realize that his
inner transformation was connected with the far-reach-
ing transformation of the world. Neither he nor the
world could resolve its dilemmas without an acceptance
of the new, because "you can't go home again."

In the last years of Wolfe's life the Wachovia
Bank in Asheville brought suit against his mother and
her family, and they were in danger of losing their
house and property. Renouncing all claim to his maternal inheritance, Wolfe gave his sister concrete advice
about reaching an agreement with the lawyers over
elastic terms such as "contingency basis." He reassured
his mother:

There is no use in going over the mistakes that were made in the past and in regretting what might have been if people had only acted differently. For my part, I can assure you that I have no feeling of bitterness and do not propose to pass judgment on what is over and done. I only hope that in the future everyone will profit from experience of the past, and try to manage things better.[12]

Not being able to deal with the past, learning nothing for the future, staring helplessly backward as if under a spell—these were for Wolfe the identifying characteristics of the truly ruined, "the lost." He felt sorry for the poor, defeated people he saw in Asheville in the summer of 1937, and for the ruined, impoverished town. In letters, conversations, and books he interpreted the greatest discovery of his life: one must make one's daily decisions as a real person in a real world because "you can't go home again." In 1938 he wrote to his sister: "Don't live in the past in a sad defeated way. We've got our own home to find or make, and our home is in the future."[13]

Wolfe received a letter from someone who had read *The Story of a Novel* accusing Wolfe of anti-semitism. The letter also said insulting things about Southerners. In a letter of reply he never mailed, Wolfe denied that his little book held "any trace of that hostile and ugly feeling which, I am sure, we both abhor" and expressed his belief in a "spirit of racial liberty and tolerance" and the hope that it might someday become universal. Perhaps Wolfe did not mail his reply because he realized the uselessness of speaking of tolerance and racial liberty to an intolerant person. In *The Web and the Rock* he handled Jewish characters neither better nor worse than members of his own family or the citizens of his home town. Indeed, some chapters show a strong sensitivity to Jewish culture. His characterization of Mr. Rosen is a tribute to his Jewish friends. His portraits of Aline Bernstein are seen through the eyes of a lover.

In the chapter of *You Can't Go Home Again* entitled "The Capture," Wolfe wrote a moving declaration of support for the oppressed and persecuted of all races and nationalities. The chapter commemorates a Jewish traveling companion who failed in his attempt to escape from Germany:

As the car in which he had been riding slid by, he lifted his pasty face and terror-stricken eyes, and for a moment his lips were stilled of their anxious pleading. He looked once, directly and steadfastly, at his former companions, and they at him. And in that gaze there was all the unmeasured weight of man's mortal anguish. George and the others felt somehow naked and ashamed, and somehow guilty. They all felt that they were saying farewell, not to a man, but to humanity; not to some pathetic stranger, some chance acquaintance of the voyage, but to mankind; not to some nameless cipher out of life, but to the fading image of a brother's face.[14]

Wolfe wanted to make up his own mind about what was going on in Germany. He studied it, uninfluenced by prejudice or other people's opinions—though we should not forget that he had always found Germany a wonderful country and the Germans a great people. With the neutrality of an experienced observer he recognized and identified what was going on:

For the first time in his life he had come upon something full of horror that he had never known before—something that made all the swift violence and passion of America, the gangster compacts, the sudden killings, the harshness and corruption that infested portions of American business and public life, seem innocent beside it. What George began to see was a picture of a great people who had been physically wounded and were now desperately ill with some dread malady of the soul.[15]

Because of his "realization," Wolfe's interest in world events increased enormously in the last years of his life. In reply to a questionnaire by *The Nation* on how the United States might keep out of war, he wrote, in March 1938, a position paper that demonstrates his acute observation and farsightedness:

The wheels of a great war machine, such as that which Germany has today, are not going to be stopped, once they have begun to roll, by a handful of reproving phrases, or by a batch of diplomatic protests. Just as the foundations of Fascism are rooted in the hopelessness and despair of a bankrupt and defeated people who, having nothing more to lose, submit to any promises of gain—this would have been apparent to anyone who visited Germany as I did in 1928 and 1930—so does the success and growth of Fascism depend upon submission, and flourish upon compromise and vacillation.[16]

Wolfe has also been accused of sympathy for fascism, as Betty Thompson mentions in her article "Thomas Wolfe: Two Decades of Criticism" (1950), but this has never been substantiated. In a letter to Perkins describing his visit to William E. Dodd, the then American ambassador in Berlin, who had a great liking for Wolfe, he said: "I wish you could have been there the other night in his house when he came back from attending Hitler's two hour and forty minute speech which was delivered to that group of automatic dummies that now bears the ironical title of 'Reichstag.' "[17] He called Dodd's home in Berlin "a free and fearless harbor for people of all opinions" and said that people who lived and walked in terror were able to draw their breath there without fear and to speak their minds. He described fascism as "a creature that thrives but is not appeased by compromise." So he found it hard to understand that people should be surprised by the facts or by Hitler's lust for power. "Where have these surprised people been living for the past ten years? If anyone ever furnished the world with a blueprint of his intentions in advance, it was Adolf Hitler."[18]

Anyone familiar with Wolfe's letters and magazine articles will recognize his acumen as an observer of the contemporary political scene. His notes on world politics, sketchily set down while he was working on his novels, stand out in the statements of those troubled times for their clarity and cogency. When powerful forces in America were militating for the principle of "isolationism," for "letting Europe fight its own wars," he wrote:

. . . "isolation" is a rhetorical concept, useful to politicians for the purpose of strengthening their majorities at home and of reassuring their constituencies, and perhaps useful to other people who project the metaphysical idea that it is possible for a nation of one hundred and thirty million people to live sealed up hermetically in peace in a world that is ravaged by war. Beyond this, I do not believe "isolation" has any real meaning in fact, because it has no existence in reality.[19]

Neither events nor the shillyshallying of the democratic powers weakened Wolfe's belief in the possibility of their acting collectively or destroyed his faith in their power to act effectively, as sooner or later they would have to do. In fact, subjugated Germany, where the truth could no longer even be whispered—a fact of life that was difficult for non-Germans to grasp—reinforced his faith in America. In *You Can't Go Home Again*, he wrote:

So, then to every man his chance—to every man the right to live, to work, to be himself, and to become whatever thing his manhood and his vision can combine to make him—this, seeker, is the promise of America.[20]

Wolfe's very love for America required him to reflect upon its weaknesses and idiosyncrasies. His criticism included self-criticism. George Webber in *You Can't Go Home Again* knows that he is not one of those intellectuals who confine himself to cliques and are disinclined to admit failure. In years of loneliness he strips himself down to "the brutal facts of self and work." Wolfe learned incessantly from his own experience. He looked closely at life and prided himself on carefully sorting out his experiences.

During the 1930s the artist in America was confronted by a dilemma: Should he submit to tradition and accept false rules of propriety for literature, as Van Wyck Brooks accused Mark Twain of doing? Or should he maintain his artistic integrity and resign himself to obscurity and poverty? George Webber complains that the literary market forces the artist either to be penni-

less like James Joyce or to write "acceptable things"
—in other words, to become "one of the little magazine
precious boys." Wolfe wrote to Hamilton Basso, the
author of the highly praised novel *The View from
Pompey's Head*, that the artist would continue to create
new forms of art and to enrich life with new creations
as long as there was either life or art.

He thought he had discovered a curious and
baffling paradox: that, despite the commonly held
image of the American as being rootless, indifferent to
convention, enterprising and progressive, the American
mentality has a tendency to become more conventional
and more rigid than the mentality of other nationalities.
In his opinion, the usual explanations—Puritanism and
Babbitry—are effects rather than causes. These effects
are connected with what he saw as other effects, though
the connection is generally overlooked: the dryness of
the American, his prognathous jaw and sharp features,
his way of walking and moving, the "kind of meager-
ness around the hips," the nasal voice, the dry precision
of his speech. The whole matter is "a thorny paradox."

The explanation Wolfe proposes is that Americans
are "surveyors." They have the resourcefulness of a
people that had to meet emergencies, fence in a patch
of wilderness and build a house, repair a mowing machine. Admirable as all this may be, it is "surveyor-
dom" rather than "exploration." The Americans' fear
of essential exploration, he says, "may be the natural
response of people who had to settle down and give
their lives some precise and formal definition in that
enormous vacancy."[21]

Comparing the ending of *You Can't Go Home Again* with certain passages from letters written while Wolfe was at college, in which he accused his countrymen of worshiping their bank accounts and considering someone a great man just because he had sold more pills than his competitors, one sees how he has closed the circle. His outspoken criticism of the people who shout "Progress, Progress, Progress" is counterbalanced by his confession of faith, the memorable "Promise of America."

America too was sick—but not done for. "America was young, America was still the New World of mankind's hope, . . . America was still resilient, still responsive to a cure—if only—if only—men could somehow cease to be afraid of truth."[22] Wolfe set down his creed. According to the French philosopher Jacques Maritain, the force that the future exerts upon America is something new in human history and an undeniable element in American greatness. Wolfe possessed this "openness to the future." As an American he had faith in it. Having made his way into the wide world from a little mountain town, he never accepted resignation or defeat. He lived his life according to the law of change and growth. "I think the enemy is here before us with a thousand faces, but I think we know that all his faces wear one mask. I think the enemy is single selfishness and compulsive greed. I think the enemy is blind, but has the brutal power of his blind grab."[23]

The story of the restlessly seeking, wandering genius in *You Can't Go Home Again* ends with Web-

ber's farewell to his beloved old friend Foxhall Edwards. The melancholy, portentous words hint that the
end is not far off—just as Wolfe's last letter to the real-
life Fox, Max Perkins, did.

Something has spoken to me in the night, burning the tapers of
the waning year; something has spoken in the night, and told
me I shall die, I know not where. Saying:

"To lose the earth you know, for greater knowing; to lose the
life you have, for greater life; to leave the friends you loved, for
greater loving; to find a land more kind than home, more large
than earth—

"—Whereon the pillars of this earth are founded, toward which
the conscience of the world is tending—a wind is rising, and the
rivers flow."[24]

You Can't Go Home Again offers touching proof
that in his own unconventional way Wolfe was a deeply
religious man, though he rejected "churchiness" and
hypocritical piety. He lived and suffered as "God's
Lonely Man" (the title of the confessional essay on
loneliness and the lonely and on Job that he rewrote so
many times). His tragedy was that he did not trust love
to dissolve and overcome the lonely man's loneliness. If
he had lived longer, he would probably have made this
"realization" too. We do not know. His last letters to
his family, which have the ring of a new beginning but
also of an imminent end, confirm what his friends said:
Wolfe was lonely.

Loneliness neither distracted nor embittered him,
for he believed that "the lonely man, who is also the
tragic man, is invariably the man who loves life dearly

—which is to say the joyful man."[25] He saw no paradox in this. Wolfe was lonely, but, as his editor Aswell said, "it was at the end a wise and friendly sort of loneliness, a self-contained loneliness, a loneliness that had long since accepted loneliness as the inescapable condition of his life."[26]

Wolfe was a person in search of something, a powerful voice proclaiming his yearning, as well as the ceaseless flow of time, which carries all mortals along with it. "Death the proud brother" was to come tragically early. Wolfe's most brilliant chapters describe dying: the hard death of young Ben, who has not yet lived, and the death of old Gant, who never succeeded in carving his unexpressible message in stone—a wanderer passing by. His son Eugene, like his creator Tom, established signs, discovered the language of symbols: a leaf, a stone, a door. In articulating his intuition about the relationship of life to death and death to life, Wolfe wrote meaningfully about what is perhaps the greatest theme in literature.

7

The Hills Beyond

The $Hills$ $Beyond$, published in 1941, contains a fragment of a novel "The Hills Beyond" and short pieces. Like many of Wolfe's works, this fragment had a long genesis, the history of which corroborates Aswell's statement that Wolfe had his own methods of writing. "Studying the mass of his manuscript was something like excavating the site of ancient Troy. One came upon evidence of entire civilizations buried and forgotten at different levels."[1] Yet in his extraordinary weaving together of rewritten sections Wolfe never overlooked a single strand. When the time came, he would dip into his famous packing case and bring out the necessary skeins. When he was working on "The October Fair" he was already planning his next book, "The Hills beyond Pentland," the story of his maternal ancestors. During the period of "realization," when he abandoned Gantism, he drew heavily on the Pentland material for his other novels. While incorporating previously written material, Wolfe continued to write new sections. In his last work, "The Hills Beyond," only one chapter—"The Bell Strikes Three"—was written as early as 1936. Historically the fragmentary "Hills Beyond" breaks off about 1880; The Web and the $Rock$ begins with Webber's birth in 1900. The part Wolfe did not live to write would have dealt with the twenty years in between.

"The Hills Beyond" is a good example of how Wolfe disregarded the standard novelistic technique of weaving an intricate structure culminating in boy getting girl. Instead, he simply adds one incident on to another. This is an essayistic technique: what he himself called "telling all about it." The poetic colors in "The Hills Beyond" are less vivid, the style less brilliant. As Aswell said, in some places the style is lean and bare.

No one can know how this family chronicle would have looked if Wolfe had revised and completed it. In its existing form it suggests that in reaction to criticism he was trying too hard to curb his exuberance, tone down the colors. He may also have been handicapped by not being able to use the protagonist of his earlier novels as "a pebble in the pool" for describing the pre-1900 period (before either Webber or he himself was born) or as a means of bringing people and landscapes to life.

The great theme of the bitter shortness of man's days is recapitulated in the last paragraph of the book, a lyrical paraphrase of the dream of time:

And time still passing . . . passing like a leaf . . . time passing, fading like a flower . . . time passing like a river flowing . . . time passing . . . and remembered suddenly, like the forgotten hoof and wheel. . . .

Time passing as men pass who never will come back again . . . and leaving us, Great God, with only this . . . knowing that this earth, this time, this life, are stranger than a dream.[2]

These are the last words on the last page. Goal-directed as he was, Wolfe would certainly have picked up the thread again. But when and how? His great packing case was full of material waiting to be integrated into a wider context and a new form. The trip he made just before his death renewed old family bonds, suggested new subjects, and gave him a new impetus.

Aswell and Perkins, Wolfe's literary executors, made a careful selection from his unpublished writings for the collection *The Hills Beyond*. They were both mindful of Wolfe's stature. The episode described in "Gentlemen of the Press" recalls Wolfe's Brooklyn period and his plan to write a book about nighttime in America. The chapter is distinguished for its well defined city-room characters and controversial social criticism.

Aswell called "Chickamauga" one of the best stories Tom ever wrote. It was written after his reconciliatory visit home in 1937, when he went back to the mountains and met a relative of his mother. "I got the idea for it from an old, old man, my great-uncle, John Westall, who lives over in Yancey County and who is ninety-five years old," he wrote to Hamilton Basso.[3] This old man described the savage Civil War battle of Chickamauga so vividly and pugently that Wolfe could hardly wait to write it down. "My idea was simply to tell the story of a great battle in the language of a common soldier." Although the story takes in the whole Civil War, as well as the life of a common soldier and his account of one of the bloodiest battles in world history, and although "it simply crackled with action from the first line," it was a long time before it was accepted—and then Wolfe received for it modest payment.

"The Return of the Prodigal," the story of Wolfe's return to Asheville, consists of two parts. The first is an imaginative account, written in 1934, of how the reviled writer goes home for one night—a night of

storm and fog. The second describes how everyone
wants to shake hands with the local celebrity—as his
mother had once prophesied they would. Literary critics will find it suggestive that the first part, like some of
the letters Wolfe wrote while he was at college, already
expresses his life maxim: you can't go home again.
Elizabeth Nowell described how Wolfe seized upon this
phrase when Ella Winter used it in a conversation with
him in 1937.[4]

The subject of "Portrait of a Literary Critic" is
readily identifiable as the critic Henry Seidel Canby. As
Aswell says, "The Lion at Morning," written about
1936, is a masterful character study that illustrates
Wolfe's humorous, incorruptible way of ascertaining a
man's inmost moods and thoughts simply by watching
him get up in the morning, eat breakfast, and read the
paper.

The confessional essay "God's Lonely Man,"
which went through many drafts before attaining its final
form, is a key to Wolfe's religiosity and basic sense of
life. Like Chekhov, Wolfe was always conscious of
man's loneliness. It should be added that while this
essay certainly deals with the sediment left by rich experience of life and the world, it does not reflect the
new-born mood of the last months of his life, when he
felt "as if a great window had been opened on life."

What do we actually know of his plans? After
joining Harpers, he wrote in a letter to Mary Louise
Aswell that he had a feeling of absolute loneliness, yet
also of a new beginning, as though a new world stood

before him. This new world seemed to be within his grasp when the time came for him to go on his trip to the west. He looked back, liberated from feuds and temptation. Like a mountain climber, he could now see direction and distances in perspective.

After reading the manuscript of *The Web and the Rock*, which Wolfe had compared to the bones of a great prehistoric animal, Aswell sent him an enthusiastic telegram saying the book was "magnificent in scope and design." His praise acted like a stimulating injection to Wolfe, who wrote to Margaret Roberts: "With this wonderful assurance I'm going back and try to live up to it until it's finished as I want it."[5] And indeed he gave of his best, making no concessions to the pressure of time.

The last letter he ever wrote is a memorable one. It proves the greatness and humility, the maturity and honesty, of this man who was not yet thirty-eight years old. Putting aside their differences and quarrels, he reminded Max Perkins, his fatherly friend and mentor, of their reunion when he had come home to find his second book a success. His sister Mabel smuggled the letter out of the hospital. "I've made a long voyage and been to a strange country," he wrote, "and I've seen the dark man very close; and I don't think I was too much afraid of him, but so much of mortality still clings to me—I wanted most desperately to live and still do." Although he knew now that he was just a grain of dust, he knew too that he was a better and a wiser man. "If I get on my feet, I'll come back."[6] Are there any signs to indicate the direction Wolfe might have taken in the future that was not granted to him? He might, for one, have taken George Webber from the point at which *You Can't Go Home Again* ends to and perhaps beyond the time of World War II. Certainly Wolfe would have found World War II as meaningful a subject as the great depression. It seems likely that this great story-teller would have continued his chronicle of his life and times.

After completing the Webber-Joyner cycle, he might have gone on to a critical, satirical treatment of the law, lawyers, and judicial processes. A fragment on this subject, written with lofty, subtle incisiveness and enlivened by a note of humor, gives us an idea of how this might have turned out. The fragment is entitled "Justice Is Blind," and it was first published in *The Enigma of Thomas Wolfe: Biographical and Critical Selections* (1953, edited by Richard Walser). A book about justice and pettifogging lawyers would have provided a change of theme while still continuing the story of his life. He wanted to work up the distressing experience of his four lawsuits into a book that would really make a stir, and it is a great pity that he did not live to do so. His genial indignation would probably have helped him to shake off all inhibitions about trying to write in the Wolfean manner without being Thomas Wolfe. A letter he wrote in 1938 jokes about "the grand old national pastime of shaking-down" and "the weaving of that unreal spider's web that is the law."[7]

Wolfe might also have written a book about his mother; he once mentioned this idea to Perkins. Perhaps he would have returned to the theme of life and work in nighttime America that fascinated him for many years. Fragments on this subject survive or were incorporated into his later works.

Wolfe's chief characteristic was his feeling that he had a message, that he could not repress his writing, that flight and compromise were unthinkable.

The course of the last two years of Wolfe's life suggests that he would have come closer and closer to his goal of truth and honesty. "I had not yet learned that one cannot really be superior without humility and tolerance and human understanding," he had written in *You Can't Go Home Again*.[8]

"That is how it has always been with me. I could never learn anything except the hard way. I must experience it for myself before I knew."[9] His angel held him tightly by the hand, as the literary critic Benno Reifenberg said. His greatness—to give it its right name—lay in his humility and his courage, his awareness of the vanity of life, and his extraordinary fortitude. "Man was born to live, to suffer, and to die, and what befalls him is a tragic lot. There is no denying this in the final end. *But we must, dear Fox, deny it all along the way*."[10]

Notes

In Retrospect

1. *Thomas Wolfe's Letters to His Mother*, ed. John S. Terry (New York: Charles Scribner's Sons, 1943), pp. 75, 50.
2. Thomas Wolfe, *From Death to Morning* (New York: Charles Scribner's Sons, 1935), p. 14.
3. Ibid., p. 109.
4. Ibid., p. 107.
5. *Letters to His Mother*, p. 79.
6. *The Letters of Thomas Wolfe*, ed. Elizabeth Nowell (New York: Charles Scribner's Sons, 1956), p. 733.
7. Ibid., p. 737.
8. Ibid., p. 589.
9. Ibid., p. 762.

1. Plays—And an Epic Touch

1. Thomas Wolfe, *Look Homeward, Angel* (New York: Charles Scribner's Sons, 1957), p. 1.
2. *Thomas Wolfe's Letters to His Mother*, ed. John S. Terry (New York: Charles Scribner's Sons, 1943), p. xvi.
3. *The Letters of Thomas Wolfe*, ed. Elizabeth Nowell (New York: Charles Scribner's Sons, 1956), p. 41.
4. Ibid., p. 39.

5. Ibid., p. 31.

6. *Thomas Wolfe's Purdue Speech "Writing and Living"*, ed. William Braswell and Leslie A. Field (Lafayette, Indiana: Purdue University Studies, 1964), p. 46.

7. *Letters of Thomas Wolfe*, p. 384.

8. Ibid., p. 57.

9. *Letters to His Mother*, p. 19.

10. Thomas Wolfe, *Mannerhouse* (New York: Harper & Brothers, 1948), pp. 143, 162, 134.

11. *Letters of Thomas Wolfe*, p. 104.

12. Thomas Wolfe, *Of Time and the River* (New York: Charles Scribner's Sons, 1935), p. 549.

13. Ibid., p. 545.

14. *Letters of Thomas Wolfe*, p. 104.

15. Thomas Wolfe, *The Story of a Novel* (New York: Charles Scribner's Sons, 1936), p. 29.

16. Ibid., p. 32.

17. Ibid., p. 35.

18. *Letters to His Mother*, p. 122.

19. *Of Time and the River*, p. 908.

20. Elizabeth Nowell, *Thomas Wolfe* (New York: Doubleday & Co., 1960), p. 103.

2. *Behind the Wall:* Look Homeward, Angel

1. *The Letters of Thomas Wolfe*, ed. Elizabeth Nowell (New York: Charles Scribner's Sons, 1956), p. 168.

2. Ibid., p. 169.

3. Thomas Wolfe, *Look Homeward, Angel* (New York: Charles Scribner's Sons, 1957), p. 118.

4. *Letters of Thomas Wolfe*, p. 111.

5. Ibid., p. 122.

6. Ibid., p. 112.

7. *Thomas Wolfe's Letters to His Mother*, ed. John S. Terry (New York: Charles Scribner's Sons, 1943), p. 50.

8. *Letters of Thomas Wolfe*, p. 130.
9. Ibid., p. 132.
10. Ibid., p. 123.
11. Ibid., p. 108.
12. Ibid., p. 732.
13. *Look Homeward, Angel*, epigraph.
14. Ibid., p. 590.
15. *Letters of Thomas Wolfe*, p. 317.
16. Ibid., p. 592.
17. Thomas Wolfe, *The Story of a Novel* (New York: Charles Scribner's Sons, 1936), pp. 8–9.
18. *Letters of Thomas Wolfe*, p. 587.
19. Thomas Wolfe, *The Web and the Rock* (New York: Harper & Brothers, 1939), p. 556.
20. *Letters of Thomas Wolfe*, p. xvii.
21. Ibid., p. 311.
22. *Letters to His Mother*, p. x.
23. *Letters of Thomas Wolfe*, p. 315.

3. Of Time and the River

1. Thomas Wolfe, *The Story of a Novel* (New York: Charles Scribner's Sons, 1936), p. 54.
2. Ibid., p. 73.
3. Ibid., p. 83.
4. *The Letters of Thomas Wolfe*, ed. Elizabeth Nowell (New York: Charles Scribner's Sons, 1956), p. 236.
5. Ibid., p. 323.
6. Thomas Wolfe, *Of Time and the River* (New York: Charles Scribner's Sons, 1935), p. 595.
7. Ibid., p. 571.
8. *Letters of Thomas Wolfe*, p. 643.
9. Ibid., p. 438.
10. Ibid., p. 722.
11. *Thomas Wolfe's Letters to His Mother*, ed. John S. Terry (New York: Charles Scribner's Sons, 1943), pp. 333–34.

4. *The Last Years*

1. *The Letters of Thomas Wolfe*, ed. Elizabeth Nowell (New York: Charles Scribner's Sons, 1956), p. 587.
2. Ibid., p. 580.
3. Ibid., p. 578.
4. Ibid., p. 655.
5. Ibid.
6. Ibid.
7. Ibid., p. 719.
8. Ibid., pp. 769–75.

5. The Web and the Rock

1. *The Letters of Thomas Wolfe*, ed. Elizabeth Nowell (New York: Charles Scribner's Sons, 1956), p. 711.
2. Ibid., p. 714.
3. Ibid.
4. Thomas Wolfe, *The Hills Beyond* (New York: Harper & Brothers, 1941), p. 371.
5. John Hall Wheelock, ed., *Editor to Author: The Letters of Maxwell E. Perkins* (New York: Charles Scribner's Sons, 1950), p. 297.
6. *The Hills Beyond*, Afterword, pp. 374–75.
7. Thomas Wolfe, *The Web and the Rock* (New York: Harper & Brothers, 1939), p. 546.
8. Ibid., p. 555.
9. Ibid., p. 686.
10. Ibid., pp. 522–23.
11. Ibid., p. 693.
12. Ibid., pp. 694–95.
13. Ibid., p. 693.

6. You Can't Go Home Again

1. Günther Blöcker, *Die neuen Wirklichkeiten.*
2. *The Letters of Thomas Wolfe,* ed. Elizabeth Nowell (New York: Charles Scribner's Sons, 1956), p. 714.
3. Ibid., p. 287.
4. Ibid., p. 715.
5. Thomas Wolfe, *You Can't Go Home Again* (New York: Harper & Brothers, 1940), pp. 246–49.
6. *Letters of Thomas Wolfe,* p. 467.
7. Thomas Wolfe, *The Story of a Novel* (New York: Charles Scribner's Sons, 1936), p. 60.
8. *Letters of Thomas Wolfe,* pp. 520–21.
9. Ibid., pp. 311–12.
10. Ibid., p. 553.
11. *You Can't Go Home Again,* p. 54.
12. *Thomas Wolfe's Letters to His Mother,* ed. John S. Terry (New York: Charles Scribner's Sons, 1943), p. 347.
13. *Letters of Thomas Wolfe,* p. 761.
14. *You Can't Go Home Again,* p. 699.
15. Ibid., p. 631.
16. *Letters of Thomas Wolfe,* p. 735.
17. Ibid., p. 461.
18. Ibid., p. 735.
19. Ibid.
20. *You Can't Go Home Again,* p. 508.
21. *Letters of Thomas Wolfe,* p. 633.
22. *You Can't Go Home Again,* p. 730.
23. Ibid., pp. 741–42.
24. Ibid., p. 743.
25. Thomas Wolfe, *The Hills Beyond* (New York: Harper & Brothers, 1941), p. 190.
26. Ibid., p. 381.

7. The Hills Beyond

1. Thomas Wolfe, *The Hills Beyond* (New York: Harper & Brothers, 1941), Afterword, p. 369.
2. Ibid., p. 348.
3. *The Letters of Thomas Wolfe*, ed. Elizabeth Nowell (New York: Charles Scribner's Sons, 1956), p. 625.
4. Elizabeth Nowell, *Thomas Wolfe* (Garden City, N. Y.: Doubleday & Co., 1960), p. 410.
5. *Letters of Thomas Wolfe*, p. 776.
6. Ibid., p. 777.
7. Ibid., p. 720.
8. Thomas Wolfe, *You Can't Go Home Again* (New York: Harper & Brothers, 1940), p. 722.
9. Ibid., p. 726.
10. Ibid., p. 737.

Bibliography

Works by Thomas Wolfe

*The Return of Buck Gavin: The Tragedy of a Mountain Out-
    law*. In *Carolina Folk Plays*, series 2. 1924.
Look Homeward, Angel: A Story of the Buried Life. 1929.
A Portrait of Bascom Hawke. 1932.
From Death to Morning. 1935.
*Of Time and the River: A Legend of Man's Hunger in His
    Youth*. 1935.
The Story of a Novel. 1936.
The Web and the Rock. 1939.
A Note on Experts: Dexter Vespasian Joyner. 1939.
*The Face of a Nation: Poetical Passages from the Writings of
    Thomas Wolfe*. 1939.
You Can't Go Home Again. 1940.
The Hills Beyond. 1941.
Gentlemen of the Press. 1942.
Thomas Wolfe's Letters to His Mother. Edited by John S. Terry.
    1943.
Stories by Thomas Wolfe. 1944.
A Stone, A Leaf, A Door: Poems by Thomas Wolfe. Edited by
    J. S. Barnes. 1946.
The Portable Thomas Wolfe. Edited by Maxwell Geismar. 1946.
Mannerhouse. 1948.
A Western Journal: A Daily Log of the Great Parks Trip. 1951.

The Correspondence of Thomas Wolfe and Homer Andrew Watt. 1954.

The Letters of Thomas Wolfe. Edited by Elizabeth Nowell. 1956.

The Short Novels of Thomas Wolfe. 1961.

The Thomas Wolfe Reader. Edited by C. Hugh Holman. 1962.

The Notebooks of Thomas Wolfe. 1970.

Works about Thomas Wolfe

Austin, N. F. *A Biography of Thomas Wolfe.* Austin, Texas: Roger Beacham Publisher, 1968.

Field, Leslie A., ed. *Thomas Wolfe: Three Decades of Criticism.* New York: New York University Press, 1968.

Fisher, V. *Thomas Wolfe as I Knew Him, and Other Essays.* Chicago: The Swallow Press, 1963.

Holman, C. Hugh. *Thomas Wolfe.* Minneapolis: University of Minnesota, 1960.

Johnson, E. D. *Of Time and Thomas Wolfe: A Bibliography, with a Character Index of His Works.* New York: Scarecrow Press, 1959.

————. *Thomas Wolfe: A Checklist.* Kent, Ohio: Kent State University Press, 1970.

McElderry, Bruce R. *Thomas Wolfe.* New York: Twayne Publishers, 1964.

Modern Fiction Studies 11, no. 3 (1965). Special Wolfe issue.

Muller, Herbert J. *Thomas Wolfe.* New York: New Directions, 1947.

Nowell, Elizabeth. *Thomas Wolfe.* Garden City, N. Y.: Doubleday & Company, 1960.

Preston, G. R. *Thomas Wolfe: A Bibliography.* New York: C. F. Boesen, 1943. Special printing.

Raynolds, R. *Thomas Wolfe: Memoir of a Friendship.* Austin, Texas: University of Texas Press, 1965.

Rubin, Louis D., Jr. *Thomas Wolfe: The Weather of His Youth.* Baton Rouge: Louisiana State University Press, 1955.

Thompson, Betty. "Thomas Wolfe: Two Decades of Criticism."
    South Atlantic Quarterly 49 (July 1950): 378–92.
Turnbull, Andrew. *Thomas Wolfe*. New York: Charles Scrib-
    ner's Sons, 1967.
Walser, Richard, ed. *The Enigma of Thomas Wolfe: Biographi-
    cal and Critical Selections*. Cambridge, Massachusetts: Har-
    vard University Press, 1953.
———. *Thomas Wolfe: An Introduction and Interpretation*.
    New York: Barnes & Noble, 1961.
Watkins, Floyd C. *Thomas Wolfe's Characters: Portraits from
    Life*. Norman, Oklahoma: University of Oklahoma, 1957.
Wheaton, Mabel Wolfe, and Blythe, LeGette. *Thomas Wolfe
    and His Family*. Garden City, N. Y.: Doubleday & Com-
    pany, 1961.
Wheelock, John Hall, ed. *Editor to Author: The Letters of Max-
    well E. Perkins*. New York: Charles Scribner's Sons, 1950.

Index